The
Men's Program

The Men's Program

A Peer Education Guide to Rape Prevention,

Third Edition

John D. Foubert

Routledge
Taylor & Francis Group

NEW YORK AND HOVE

Published in 2005 by
Brunner-Routledge
Taylor & Francis Group
270 Madison Avenue
New York, NY 10016

Published in Great Britain by
Brunner-Routledge
Taylor & Francis Group
27 Church Road
Hove, East Sussex BN3 2FA

Printed in the United States of America on acid-free paper
10 9 8 7 6 5 4 3 2 1

International Standard Book Number-10: 0-415-95174-7 (Softcover)
International Standard Book Number-13: 978-0-415-95174-6 (Softcover)
Library of Congress Card Number 2004065144

Library of Congress Cataloging-in-Publication Data

Foubert, John
    The Men's Program : a peer education guide to rape prevention / John D. Foubert.--3rd ed.
        p. cm.
    Reprint. Originally published as The Men's Program. 3rd ed. Holmes Beach, Fla : Learning Publications, c2003.
    Includes bibliographical references.
    ISBN 0-415-95174-7 (alk. paper)
    1. Rape--Prevention--Study and teaching. 2. Male college students--Counseling of. 3. Peer counseling of students. I. Title.

HV6558.F68 2005
362.883--dc22   2004065144

Taylor & Francis Group is the Academic Division of T&F Informa plc.

Visit the Taylor & Francis Web site at
http://www.taylorandfrancis.com
and the Brunner-Web site at
http://www.routledgementalhealth.com

Contents

Introduction.. xi

1 What Is *The Men's Program*? 1

The Program Begins • The Video • Helping a Survivor • Other Ways Men Can Prevent Rape • Why *The Men's Program* is So Effective • Ordering the Video • The Script

2 Presenting "The Men's Program" 7

How To Help a Sexual Assault Survivor: What Men Can Do • Disclaimer • Overview • Definition Poster • Helping a Survivor • Medical and Safety Needs • No More Violence • Listen • Believe Her • Help Her Regain Control • Realize Limitations • Other Ways Men Can Help End Rape • Communicate During Encounters • Cooperation Does Not Equal Consent • The Freeze • Stop, Ask, Clarify • Help Change Social Norms

3 A Training Course for Peer Educators 21

Comprehensive Design for the Course • Enrollment • Theoretical and Practical Perspectives on Being a Sexual-Assault Peer Educator • Assigned Readings • Books • Course Packet Containing the Following Articles • Course Goals • Course Evaluation • Course Outline • Assignments • Class Participation • Journals • Interview • Choice A • Choice B • Experiential Learning Project • Practice Presentation • Personal Goal Statement for Presentations • Presentation • Final Exam • Class-by-Class Descriptions • Belief-System Theory • The Elaboration-Likelihood Model

4 Recruiting Men to Be Peer Educators 55

Step One: Solicit Nominations • Step Two: Reach Out to Nominees • Step Three: Schedule an Interview • Step Four: Conduct the Interview • Step Five: Decide Whether or Not to Admit Him

5 Advice for Peer Educators from Men Who Have Been There 59

Advice from a Man Who Walked the Walk by Steve McAllister • Finding a Cause by Ben Jamieson • Educate Yourself, Support Others • Communicate During Encounters • Tough Work

6 Resources for Advisors and Sample "One in Four" Constitution....................... 69

Sample Press Release for Debut of a "One in Four" Chapter • Male Student Leaders at UVA Unite to Educate Peers About Rape • Sample Statement for "One in Four" President to Make at a Debut Performance Open to Both Men and Women • Sample Agenda for a Beginning of the Year Retreat • Sample Mission Statement for a "One in Four" Chapter • Sample–"One in Four" Constitution/Bylaws • Preamble

Appendices.. 83

Appendix A — A Summary of Research on *The Men's Program*............................. 85

Study #1: The Effects of *The Men's Program* on Rape-Myth Acceptance Over a Two-Month Period • Key Hypotheses • Participants • Materials • Design and Procedure • Results

• Limitations • Implications • Study #2: Long-Term Effects of *The Men's Program* on Men's Rape-Myth Acceptance and Likelihood of Raping • Key Hypotheses • Participants • Materials • Design and Procedure • Results • Limitations • Implications • Study #3: The Impact of *The Men's Program* on Homophobia among College Men • Method • Results

Appendix B — Getting Off the Ground.. 93

Video Order Form

Appendix C — Handouts for the Training Class.. 101

Handout #1: Sex, Power, and Violence • Handout #2: Values Continuum for Gay, Lesbian, and Bisexual Issues • Handout #3: Hints for Reading Journal Articles • Handout #4: The Global Health Burden of Rape Summary of Main Points (1994) • Handout #5: Explaining Malamuth (1981) • Handout #6: Rape Myths: Who Believes Them? • Handout #7: *The Legal Bias Against Rape Victims* • Handout #8: Points to Emphasize from *The Legal Bias Against Rape Victims* • Handout #9: Experiential Learning Project • Handout #10: Rape-Trauma Syndrome • Handout #11: Dealing With Difficult Audience Members • Handout #12: Research and Theoretical Basis of The Men's Program • Handout #13: Difficult Questions for Peer Educators • Handout #14: How Often Does Rape Happen to Women? • Handout #15: Interesting Responses We Get from Male Audiences • Handout #16: Thoughts on Male Privilege for Men to Ponder • Handout #17: Characteristics of Offenders • Handout #18: Lecture Notes for Article by Lonsway (1996) • Handout #19: Discussion Questions for *Sexual Assault in Context* • Handout #20: Rape Myths • Handout #21: Results of a Seven-month Study of The Men's Program • Handout #22: Why Using a Male-on-Male Rape Scenario is Appropriate in Educating Men About Sexual Assault • Handout #23: How to Handle Difficult People and Questions • Handout #24: Suggested Answers for a Variety of Questions • Handout #25: Survivor Empathy • Handout #26: The Male Box

Appendix D — Sample Recruitment Materials 151

Sample Letter to Colleagues Inviting Nominations for "One in Four" Members • Sample Letter to Send to Men Nominated for Membership in "One in Four" • Attachment to Enclose With Letter to Send Men Who Agree to Interview • Sample of Letter to Send Men Who Agree to Interview • Suggested Evaluation Criteria and Scale for "One in Four" Candidates

Appendix E — *The Men's Program* Training for University Judicial Boards 157

Overview • Disclaimer • Definitions • Empathy Exercise • Rape-Trauma Syndrome • False Accusations • Characteristics of Offenders

Appendix F — Condensed Training Program for Peer Educators... 165

Training Day 1 • To-Do List to Finish Before the Spring Semester • Training Day 2 • Training Day 3

Appendix G — References 173

Acknowledgments

Since *The Men's Program* was first presented in the fall of 1993, I have benefited from the advice, criticism, wisdom, and support of individuals far too many to count or certainly to fit on these pages. My apologies to all whose names do not appear.

First, I would like to thank the men of "Stealing Home" at the University of Richmond, who first presented "The Men's Program." Next I would like to thank the men of the first "One in Four" chapter, founded in 1997 at the University of Maryland, College Park. Their foundational work in creating norms for chapters that would soon spring up all over the country has left a long and continuing legacy. Next, I would like to thank all those who helped NO MORE get off the ground—people who have served as members of the Board of Directors, the Honorary Board of Advisors, active members, and financial contributors. Each has left a mark on this growing organization.

I give tremendous thanks to Dick Ramon for his graciousness and enthusiasm for re-shooting the video. His work is the foundation for *The Men's Program*, has affected men for decades, and will for many years to come.

Next, I would like to offer my deep gratitude to the spectacular members of the "One in Four" chapter at the University of Virginia. They took the mission of "One in Four" to uncharted territory, served as the basis for many of the improvements in this new addition, and provided me with unending support, encouragement, and friendship.

Tremendous thanks to the founders of William and Mary's new "One in Four" chapter, who have gotten off to an exceptionally strong start. Their insight and dedication promises to affect future editions of this book. Their work will make a lasting and permanent difference at our *alma mater*.

Several people have contributed significant ideas and suggestions to this book. Thanks to all those who have made comments at conferences, over e-mail, and in person. Foremost among them, I thank Brad Perry for his suggestions on the entire book, for his extensive comments on the script and training exercises, and for authoring several pieces as noted throughout this new edition. I also thank him for constantly prodding me to improve my work, for his perspective on responding to critics, and for his brilliant intellect and passion that challenge me to improve my work regularly.

Significant contributions to this book were also made by Christopher Kilmartin, Alan McEvoy, Andy Oldham, Andrea Perry, James Kohl, Sharon Kirkland, Steve McAllister, and Ben Jamieson. Thanks to you all. Thanks to Brian Kraft and to James Kohl for their years of continuing service to NO MORE and moreover for their friendship. Thanks also to David Shonka for his keen insight, outstanding presenting, unwavering support, and lifelong friendship. Finally, I thank my wife Susan for being my strongest supporter, closest confidant, best friend, light of my life, and eternal love of my heart. As with all of my work, this book is dedicated to the glory of God.

About the Author

Dr. John D. Foubert received a B.A. in both Psychology and Sociology from the College of William and Mary, an M.A. in Psychology from the University of Richmond, and a Ph.D. in College Student Personnel Administration from the University of Maryland at College Park. Dr. Foubert has served as a student affairs administrator at the University of Richmond, the University of Maryland, and the University of Virginia. In 2002, he was appointed to be an assistant professor of Higher Education at the College of William and Mary where he teaches graduate students about how to be higher-education administrators and advises an all-male, sexual-assault, peer-education group, "One in Four."

Dr. Foubert is also the founder and president of NO MORE, Inc., the National Organization of Men's Outreach for Rape Education, www.nomorerape.org. NO MORE is a non-profit organization dedicated to ending rape through means shown to be most effective through scientific research studies.

In addition to being the author of *The Men's Program*, Dr. Foubert has published numerous studies about rape prevention in publications such as the *Journal of American College Health*, the *Journal of College Student Development*, *Sex Roles*, and the *NASPA Journal*. Since 1993 his work has been used by countless universities, state health departments, the U.S. Naval Academy, other military units, rape-crisis centers, police departments, and correctional facilities to educate men about rape.

An award-winning practitioner, scholar, and programmer, Dr. Foubert has been identified by the American College Personnel Association as an "Emerging Scholar" and was the runner-up for the National Dissertation of the Year Award from the National Association of Student Personnel Administrators for his work in rape prevention. His work has been covered by the *Washington Post*, numerous television news programs, and he has been a featured guest on both *Voice of America* and the National Public Radio program, *Talk of the Nation*. Dr. Foubert is a regular keynote speaker and consultant to universities, state health departments, and state sexual-assault coalitions on how to lower men's likelihood of raping.

Introduction

The Men's Program, an all-male, sexual-assault, peer-education program was developed during the fall of 1993. Since that time the program has been implemented in colleges and universities, rape-crisis centers, and military units nationwide. Implementing the program is as simple as using this manual. You might choose to present this program yourself as a professional staff member, or even better, you might choose to train a group of peer educators to present the program.

This manual begins with a complete description of what *The Men's Program* is and why it is so effective. Chapter 2 gives you a complete presentation script for peer educators (or others) to present the program. Related material is provided for you in Appendix B, which includes program processing posters, an advertising sample, and instructions for ordering the video used in this program.

Chapter 3 fully describes a three-credit class to train men to be sexual-assault peer educators. The chapter begins with a course syllabus and includes an extensive instructor's guide with course goals, assignments, and class-by-class descriptions of recommended activities. Related material in Appendix C provides you with helpful handouts for many class sessions.

Chapter 4 outlines how to recruit and select men to be in a sexual-assault, peer-education group. Related material is printed in Appendix D, including sample recruiting letters and interview questions for prospective peer educators.

Chapter 5 provides advice from former peer-educators.

Chapter 6 provides advice for advisors including a sample constitution for a sexual-assault, peer-education group.

To help substantiate your efforts, Appendix A describes two evaluation studies of *The Men's Program*. The first shows that men who see this program experience a 50 percent drop in rape-myth acceptance, and that two months later this drop remains significantly lower ($p < .001$) than their pretest levels. The second study describes how men who see this program experience a significant drop in rape-myth acceptance and a significant drop in their reported likelihood of raping—effects that last for at least an entire seven-month academic year. This same study provides qualitative data supporting the program's efficacy. Having all of this information will help you and your presenters to know they truly are making a difference. In addition, you can use this research with funding and decision-making authorities on your campus or in your organization to justify the use of *The Men's Program*. This appendix also describes a study showing that *The Men's Program* has no effect on audience members' homophobic attitudes.

The members of the National Organization of Men's Outreach for Rape Education, NO MORE, are working hard to encourage universities, rape-crisis centers, the military, and high schools to include *The Men's Program* among their rape-prevention efforts. We hope you will join us.

What Is *The Men's Program*?

In *The Men's Program*, participants are taken through a workshop in which they learn what a rape feels like and how to help a woman recover from a rape experience. As this book will show you, not only do they learn how to help women recover from rape, but they become less likely to have attitudes that are false, stereotyped ways of thinking about rape (rape myths). In addition, men who see it report a lower likelihood of raping—effects that last for at least a seven-month academic year.

As you will read, *The Men's Program* is designed as an all-male workshop because research shows that all-male, peer-education programs are much more likely to change men's attitudes and behavioral intent to rape than programs presented in a coeducational format or by people who are not peers of the audience (Brecklin and Forde 2001; Earle 1996). For this reason, it is suggested that *The Men's Program* be presented by male peer educators who are members of an all-male, peer-education group advised by a male administrator, graduate student, or faculty member. However, different interests and resources available on different campuses and other settings may direct your choices. Although it is preferable to have a male advisor for a peer education group, women have done so successfully and are encouraged to start and maintain such groups, particularly when men are not readily available as advisors. A female staff or faculty member might also use the video described later in this book to have males "present" the program via video, and then discuss it and answer questions (for information on the video, see Appendix B).

The Men's Program focuses on increasing men's empathy toward women who survive rape. It convinces men that being raped is a traumatic experience and shows men how they can help women recover from the experience, if a woman comes to them asking for help. The program also leads to significant declines in men's rape-myth acceptance and behavioral intent to rape and shows men how they can change their own behavior to avoid being sexually coercive. The program format is a scripted presentation, with the central focus being a video produced by the National Organization of Men's Outreach for Rape

Education (NO MORE), that describes a rape situation. Each section of the program uses preprinted posters, overhead transparencies, or PowerPoint with pertinent information to reinforce key points. Toward the end of the program, peer educators open the floor for questions.

The Program Begins

The Men's Program opens by establishing the non-confrontational nature of the program. Peer educators give an overview of what will be covered in the subsequent hour, and make sure that everyone knows that they can leave at anytime. Peer educators then discuss the distinction between sexual assault and rape. Next, participants view a 15-minute video. Peer educators introduce the video by stating that it describes "a rape situation" that will help participants to better understand how to help a sexual-assault survivor. Participants are not told that the video describes two men raping a *male* police officer. They know only that the video "describes a rape situation."

The Video

The police trainer on the video describes an event in which a police officer encounters a situation in which he could not predict what was about to happen, was startled, gave in to a rape out of fear for losing his life, experiences a painful and degrading exam in the hospital, fears the potential of sexually transmitted infections, and endures the questions of his colleagues who wonder why he did not fight back, and their accusations that he really wanted the rape to happen.

The video shows a speech by a male police officer who describes another male police officer who is moving a trash can in an alley. Two attackers surprise him and take control of the situation. The police officer is not told to move; he quickly assesses the situation. He ends up submitting to a rape out of fear that greater harm might be done to him. Later, he endures a difficult hospital examination, becomes concerned about sexually transmitted infections, and is subjected to insensitive comments from his colleagues that perhaps he had met his attackers before and that maybe he really wanted the incident to happen. These segments of the video are processed as they relate to experiences commonly had by women who survive rape.

At the conclusion of the video, peer educators break the stunned silence by explaining that a video in which a man is raped by another man was used because it is the closest parallel available for helping men understand what it might feel like to be assaulted. The peer educators use the video to draw parallels from the police officer's experience to experiences commonly had by female survivors before, during, and after being raped.

A pair of peer educators take turns reminding the audience of several segments of the video and relating these to common experiences of women who survive rape. These common survivor experiences include having a rape happen in an everyday situation that turns bad, reacting with overwhelming fear, eventually submitting to the act to avoid further violence, worrying about long-term physical consequences, enduring a hospital examination, and suffering the questions about why she didn't resist the attack. As men are led through these parallels, they develop a deeper empathy for rape survivors. The message they receive is that rape is a violent crime that is not the fault of the survivor.

Helping a Survivor

At this point in the program, the peer educators note that one in four college women have survived rape or attempted rape since turning 14. This statistic is used to show the men that learning to help a survivor is relevant to them, as it is likely that someone they know has survived rape. Peer educators thoroughly review the importance of discussing her medical and safety needs, and of listening, believing, and accepting the survivor's decisions even if they disagree. In addition, the peer educators urge the participants to resist the temptation to ask for details about the rape, to avoid suggestions of further violence, and to recognize his and the survivor's limitations.

Other Ways Men Can Prevent Rape

The final section of the program focuses on what men could do in their own behavior to help prevent rape. During this program segment, men are encouraged to communicate openly during their own sexual encounters, to recognize that cooperation does not equal consent, and to stop, ask, and clarify when any uncertainty exists. Peer educators urge participants to educate themselves further about the sexual-assault issue, and to support other men's efforts to educate themselves. Peer educators then discuss the effects of rape jokes and the impact of sexist attitudes, and encourage men to condemn the abuse of women. Next, a question-and-answer period allows participants to request additional information or to ask for clarification of key points. After answering questions and identifying resources on campus, the program ends on a serious yet solemn tone, noting that if the hour in which the program took place was an average hour in the United States that approximately 20 women would have survived rape and other forms of sexual assault (National Crime Victimization Survey 2003).

Why *The Men's Program* is So Effective

The Men's Program offers a unique approach to the problem.

In Appendix A, you will read how research in a study of five fraternity pledge classes shows that *The Men's Program* lowered men's belief in rape myths by 50 percent, with their attitudes still being significantly improved two months later. This study included limitations, including a decline in rape-myth belief in a control group. In a later study with a larger sample and improved methods, stronger and more clearly positive results emerged. In a study of eight fraternities, men who saw *The Men's Program* were significantly less likely to believe rape myths, and were less likely to believe rape myths than a control group. This lower rape-myth belief was significant after the program was seen and on a seven-month follow-up. What is most striking was that seven months after seeing the program, men who saw the program did not have a statistically significant "rebound" in rape-myth belief. Rather, their belief in rape myths declined after seeing the program and the decline remained statistically equivalent seven months later. This is a longer effect than any other program evaluated in the research literature today. Moreover, men's self-reported likelihood of raping also significantly dropped immediately after the program and remained significantly lower (with no rebound) seven months later. While small differences involved led to the lack of a difference in the likelihood of raping between the control group and program participants seven months after the program, program participants did significantly lower their likelihood of raping and retained that decrease seven months later. Moreover, 75 percent of men who indicated some likelihood of raping before seeing the program reported lower likelihood of raping after the program and seven months later. Perhaps this is the most compelling result of all—the program reaches three-quarters of the men we are most trying to reach.

How does *The Men's Program* account for this improvement?

The Men's Program combines the characteristics that research literature shows to be the most effective with an approach to changing attitudes and behaviors that fit a well-tested theoretical model. To date, no other treatment has included the combination of techniques used by this program. *The Men's Program* uses an all-male, peer-education, victim-empathy approach. In addition, by framing the program in the context of a "how to help a sexual-assault survivor" program, the likelihood increases that men will use a type of thinking called "central-route processing." Such processing, characterized by the motivation to hear the message, the ability to understand the message, and the perceived personal relevance of the program material, has been shown to be more strongly associated with long-term attitude and behavior change (Petty and Cacioppo 1986).

By framing the workshop as a training workshop in which men learn how to help women recover from a rape experience, *The Men's Program* appeals to a "potential helper" persona, rather than the "potential rapist" persona found in most other rape-prevention approaches. In *The Men's Program*, men listen as potential helpers and are presented with information that has been shown to be most effective in content and format, making long-term changes in attitude and behavioral intent more likely. Such changes are desirable for all men, whether or not they indicate a likelihood of raping. Even those men who indicate no likelihood of raping may believe some rape myths. *The Men's Program* helps intentionally create campus climates in which there are fewer and less severe beliefs about women and rape that are sexist, stereotypical, and debilitating to the goals of egalitarian campus cultures.

The research underlying the use of *The Men's Program* includes findings by Brecklin and Forde (2001) and Earle (1996) showing that all-male, peer-education programs are more successful than mixed-gender programs and those not presented by peers. Other research has shown that as men understand rape trauma better and have more aversion to rape, they report less likelihood of raping (Hamilton and Yee 1990).

When high-risk men see a video designed to raise empathy for the survivor and are guided through scenarios depicting themselves as rape survivors, their behavioral intent to rape declines immediately after experiencing such a program (Schewe and O'Donohue 1993). *The Men's Program* adds to this a format designed to fit theories of effective attitude and behavior change and a peer-education approach along with a description of a male-on-male rape experience.

As mentioned earlier, the centerpiece of *The Men's Program* is a video from the National Organization of Men's Outreach for Rape Education (NO MORE).

Ordering the Video

This video, and one in which *The Men's Program* is presented by a team of experienced peer educators, can be ordered using the form found in Appendix B.

The Script

The script for *The Men's Program* is in Chapter 2. Sample transparencies/posters are included in Appendix B. The script is written for a peer-education group that calls themselves "One in Four." You may decide to call your group by a different name. If you would like to adopt this name for your group, and/or if you would like to affiliate with NO MORE, please contact John D. Foubert, Ph.D., President, NO MORE and Assistant Professor of Higher Education, Jones 320, William and Mary School of Education, P. O. Box 8795, Williamsburg, VA 23187, 757-221-2322, or e-mail nomore@wm.edu.

Presenting "The Men's Program"

This chapter contains the script for *The Men's Program*, also known by its more descriptive title, "How to Help a Sexual Assault Survivor: What Men Can Do." The script itself is broken down into four parts (A, B, C, and D). Within each part, it is broken down in half, with parts intended to be delivered separately by presenters who are members of "Team 1" and "Team 2." It is recommended that each peer educator spend their first semester learning to present the parts assigned to either Team 1 or Team 2. This will allow him to get to know half of the script well. Later, when more experienced, each peer educator can spend time learning the entire script.

Each presentation will require at least one peer educator from team one and at least one from Team 2. Typically, at least four peer educators are sent to each presentation. When four men are present, each peer educator presents the lines assigned to their team for 2 of the 4 parts of the program. For example one peer educator can present Team 1 Parts A and C, another can present Team 2 Parts A and C. Person three could present Team 1 Parts B and D, and person four could present Team 2 parts B and D. For larger and/or tougher audiences, you may want to send more than four presenters.

Of course, you may find that a different way of breaking up the script works for you or your group. Presenting the entire program by oneself is not unheard of, but is extremely difficult. Having at least one other person co-present allows presenters to have the script on hand and look at their next lines while the other peer educator is speaking.

While it is encouraged that peer educators stick to the script as much as possible, it is also encouraged that they adapt the language to fit their own personal style. Presenters should focus on making each point rather than on getting every word exactly as written. In addition, peer educators are particularly encouraged to weave their own personal experiences into their presentations. For example, if the peer educator has talked with a survivor before, he might include lessons he learned from this while presenting Part C (of course maintain all confidentiality). Other areas lend themselves to appropriate sharing of personal experience. Appropriate improvisations are encouraged.

Before presenting, it is important to do several things.

- Arrive early at the presentation site (at least 15-30 minutes early).

- Meet the person who invited you to present. If attendance is voluntary, encourage him or her to round up people to come down to the presentation. Offer to have some of your group help with this process.

- Have the others in your presenting group set up the TV/VCR unit. Put the video in and send a fellow peer to the back of the room to insure that the sound can be heard in the back.

- Cue the video up to the start.

- Set up chairs in the room so that every seat is facing the presentation area.

- Put resource fliers of local counseling and support services for rape survivors at the entrance/exit area of the room in which you are presenting.

- To build rapport informally chat with people as they arrive.

For a helpful example of how to present the program, a video is available from NO MORE, Inc., as described in Appendix B. The following pages contain the script for presenting "The Men's Program." Good luck.

How To Help a Sexual Assault Survivor: What Men Can Do

Part A: Introduction

Team 1

Welcome to "How to Help a Sexual Assault Survivor: What Men Can Do." We are members of "One in Four." Our name, "One in Four" comes from the statistic that *one in four* college women have survived rape or attempted rape since their fourteenth birthday. We are also the group that seeks to be the *ones who inform* other men how to help survivors recover from a rape experience. In addition, we are affiliated with an organization called NO MORE, which stands for the National Organization of Men's Outreach for Rape Education—a group that is working to end men's violence against women.

As we start off, we want to make it clear that we are not here to blame you for rape, or preach to you about it.

We are here because many women go to men after they have been sexually assaulted, and we want you to be prepared in case a woman comes to you for help or support.

So, we're not here to lecture you about why you shouldn't rape a woman. We assume you don't want to do that. Instead, we are here with a positive message. We want to teach you how you can help a woman recover from a rape experience. We want you to know how you can really make a difference. This will be our focus for the next 45 minutes.

Team 2

Disclaimer

Obviously, rape is a disturbing subject. There are parts of this program that will probably disturb you. If you have to leave during the program for any reason, that's OK. However, we do hope you will stay with us.

According to the National Crime Victimization Survey, over 90 percent of the time, rape survivors are female, and 99 percent of the time offenders are male. So, throughout the program we will refer to survivors as female and offenders as male. It's important to remember that survivors and offenders can be of either sex. As we said, the goal of our program is to teach you as men how to help women recover from rape, and that is what our focus will be.

If you are a rape survivor, or are a friend or relative of a survivor, you may be particularly upset by this program, particularly by the videotape we will show you. If you'd like to talk more privately, we will be available at the end of the program. Also, just so you know, we have placed some flyers by the door that give you an overview of resources available.

Team 1

Overview

We are going to do five basic things in this program.

- First, we will define rape.

- Next, we will show you and then discuss a police training video that describes a rape situation. This tape will help you learn about what rape is like so that you are better able to help a survivor in case she comes to you.

- We will then talk about how to help a sexual-assault survivor.

- After that we will talk about other ways you can help decrease the incidence of sexual assault.

- Finally, we will take any questions you have at the end.

Team 2

Definition Poster

To start off, we'll go over a couple definitions. [Note: you may want to insert your local definitions here instead of those printed below.]

The first definition we'd like to go over is for sexual assault. The definition we use for sexual assault is a broad one, and includes many different types of behavior. As you can see:

Sexual assault – Sexual intercourse without consent, forcible sodomy, sexual penetration with an object, intentionally touching an unwilling person's intimate parts, or forcing an unwilling person to touch another's intimate parts. These acts occur by force, threat, surprise, intimidation, or by taking advantage of someone's helplessness or inability to consent.

So basically what this definition of sexual assault includes would be having intercourse with someone who doesn't agree to it or can't agree to it. It also includes oral sex, anal sex, penetrating someone with an object, touching someone's intimate parts, or making them touch your intimate parts when they don't agree to do so and/or are forced to do so.

Rape is a more specific kind of sexual assault. The U.S. Department of Justice defines rape as:

Rape – sexual intercourse by force or against that person's will, or where the victim is incapable of giving consent given the persons age or temporary or permanent mental or physical incapacity.

So you can see that rape would be having intercourse with someone when they don't agree to it or are forced into it, or are unable to agree to it. Cases of rape also fit the broader definition of sexual assault, but not all sexual-assault cases meet the definition of rape.

Particularly in the case of rape, some people think that the most common type of rape happens when a guy a woman doesn't know grabs her by surprise and rapes her. While rape by a stranger does occur sometimes, we want you to remember this:

Four out of five times when a woman is raped, it is by someone she knows. It could be an acquaintance. It could be a friend. It could be a date. But four out of five times, it is someone she knows. And the average length of time she has known him is one year. Not just a few weeks, but on average, it's been one year.

Team 1

Right now we're going to show you a 15-minute video that describes a rape situation. This will help you understand what rape survivors go through. The tape itself is of a police detective who is training new officers about how to deal with rape situations. Again, we want to let you know that the video is graphic and disturbing. After the video is over, we'll talk more about how it feels to be raped so you can be better prepared if a woman comes to you.

[📷 Show tape here]

[After the video is finished, pause for a few seconds to allow the message to sink in to the audience.]

Part B

Team 1

We showed you this video to help you understand what it might feel like to be raped. If a woman comes to you after she has been raped, it is important that you understand what it might have felt like. Obviously, both men and women can be raped and there are differences between a man raping a woman and a man raping a man. Discussing a situation in which a man is forcibly penetrated by another man is the closest parallel we could find to help you understand what rape feels like. As with many male-on-male rapes, this video showed you a case where presumably heterosexual perpetrators used rape and battery to assert power and control over another man. Now that you've heard what rape might feel like, we are going to draw some parallels between the police officer's experience and common experiences women have before, during and after being sexually assaulted. This will help you learn more about what it feels like for women to be raped, and will make you better prepared, in case a woman comes to you.

Team 1
Police Officer's Experience

Team 2
Experiences Common to Women

A Cop Moves a Trash Can

Think back to when the police officer decided to move the trash can. He was just doing his job, in fact, he was just being helpful. It was just another normal thing he did as he went about his normal routine. Of course, he had no way to know what was about to happen.

Everyday Situation Turns Bad

In the same way, when women are raped, many of these incidents arise out of normal everyday situations. A woman may go to the room of a trusted male friend or be with a guy she's met and would like to have some form of contact with. Maybe she wanted to kiss him. But at some point, he takes control away from her. The point is that there are no big signals that a rape is about to occur, no flashing sign that goes off to say "you are about to be raped." These are just every day situations that turn bad.

"Don't Make a Move"

In the next part of the video, the police officer is told not to make a move. His first reaction, as he is being threatened, is to remain still and figure out what is going on.

Overwhelming Fear

In a similar way, a rape survivor's first instinct is to be scared and to freeze from the fear of what might happen. Usually, she's with someone that she trusts, and that trust is being grossly violated. It is very common for her first reaction to be

Get on Your Knees

Later, the police officer is told to get on his knees and it becomes more obvious what is about to happen. It's hard to tell what anyone would do in this situation, without living through it, but he decided the most important thing was to stay alive.

Fear of STIs

In this situation, the police officer worried that given the high-risk contact that was involved, that he had to worry about catching a whole variety of sexually transmitted infections.

Humiliating Hospital Visit

Remember how he felt in the waiting room? He wasn't the first one in because he wasn't a gun shot victim, and he wasn't in immediate danger of dying. He was then put on a table and had a doctor probing around his body collecting evidence. Clearly, this was an uncomfortable, humiliating exam.

to remain absolutely still, to freeze, with an overwhelming sense of fear.

Desire to Avoid Violence

Most men are larger and stronger than most women. This difference can be intimidating to many women, especially in a sexual situation where their trust is being violated. In addition, many women are raised to avoid and to calm violent situations. They may go along with what is happening to try to avoid violence to the extent possible. According to the U.S. Department of Justice, many female survivors of sexual assault do physically resist (70%), but they end up being overpowered physically or psychologically.

Fear of STIs and Pregnancy

Today, there are a lot of sexually transmitted infections to worry about. Today, being raped could mean catching a potentially fatal disease. According to the Centers for Disease Control, one out of every 500 college students is infected with HIV. In addition, one out of five adults in the United States has genital herpes.

For women survivors, there is an added risk that men don't have. Women also face the possibility that the rape could have resulted in a pregnancy. In fact, pregnancy occurs in about 5% of rape cases. These women must then consider the ramifications of that pregnancy on their lives.

Another Painful Process

Many women describe the rape exam they go through in the hospital as painful. Once more, another person is probing her body, this time to take physical evidence and treat her injuries. Have you ever asked one of your female friends what a normal gynecological exam feels like? They probably told you it can be painful. Well, a rape exam feels much worse, is much more thorough, and it happens right after one of the worst experiences of her life.

Did You Fight?

Remember how the officers reacted to the raped officer. They couldn't believe he didn't fight back. They couldn't understand that he was just trying to stay alive. They also suggested it might have happened before and maybe he really wanted it to happen.

Did You Resist?

[Increase volume steadily to a yell.] Where were you? Were you drinking? What were you wearing? Did you lead him on? Did you have sex with him before? Did you get him all worked up? Did you scream, yell? Did you scratch his eyes out? Did you just make this up? Did you really want this to happen? [Normal tone of voice.] Rape survivors get asked these questions all of the time, and none of them matter. The point is, her instinct was to stay alive and no matter what, *no one* ever asks to be raped.

Team 1

This rape experience we just described is similar to what many women experience in college. In fact, one out of every four college women have survived rape or attempted rape since they turned 14. One out of four college women have gone through an experience similar to the one we just talked about. Knowing that, what can we do?

Part C: Helping a Survivor

Team 1

Now that you've learned how rape is defined and what it might feel like to be raped, we come to the main point of our program. We are going talk about how to help a sexual-assault survivor who comes to you asking for your help. These suggestions are particularly relevant when a woman comes to you just after she has been sexually assaulted. Many of these suggestions also hold true for women who may tell you about their experience months or years later. Obviously, no woman reacts the same way to being sexually assaulted and different women find different things helpful in their recovery. We will focus on reactions that most women have and what tends to be most helpful to them if they come to you immediately after they have been raped.

Medical and Safety Needs

- **Medical** – It is important that she goes to the hospital for medical attention, particularly in the first three days after the assault. This will also allow her to save evidence, so she can decide later whether to be a witness in a criminal case against her attacker. This medical attention will include STI testing, pregnancy counseling, and treatment of her injuries. She may even have internal injuries that she cannot feel. Remember though that all you can really do is suggest that she go to the hospital and take her if she wants to go. If she doesn't want to go right away, remember that it's her choice not to go.

- **Safety** – Remember that she still may be in danger. If you can, make sure she has a safe place to stay, offer to stay with her if she wants you to, or offer to call a friend for her to stay with.

Team 2

No More Violence

- I don't know about you, but if a woman I was close to told me that a guy raped her, my first instinct would be to find that guy and end rape, starting with him. Basically, beat the snot out of him. Maybe this would be your instinct too; a lot of guys feel this way at first. However, if you think about it, the survivor has already tried to try to calm one violent man down. The last thing she needs is to feel like she has to calm you down and try to control your anger too. Saying that you are going to go beat him up is the last thing most women want to hear. She may also worry that if you beat him up, he will come back to rape her again. Instead of more violence, let her know, calmly, that you are sorry that this happened to her and that you will do anything you can to help her.

Team 1

Listen

- So as you help her, remember this simple rule: it's better to talk less and listen more.

- Don't ask for details about what she was wearing or where she was.

- Don't suggest why it happened.

- Listen to what she wants to say, and don't judge her statements.

- Also, while you are listening to her, she may want a hug, but some survivors don't want to be touched. Be sure to ask her whether she wants to be held or not, and follow her lead.

Team 2

Believe Her

- The single most important factor in a woman's recovery from rape is whether or not she is believed.

- Now, a lot of guys think that women falsely report rape all the time. They might think that it's a "he said, she said" scenario. They might think that about half the time she's telling the truth, half the time he is. We were concerned about this, so we went to the FBI for the best statistics on this. What we found was that very few rapes are false reports. According to the FBI, only 8 percent of reported rapes are false reports. To be honest, even this 8 percent number is probably inflated as it relies on the judgment of people who see evidence they believe conflicts with her story and conclude that the rape must not have happened. Of course, not all the people making these judgments do so accurately. So at a minimum, 92 percent of the time when a woman reports a rape, that is exactly what happened. Given that it is so important that she is believed, and given that it is so likely that she is telling the truth, we strongly suggest you believe her, always.

- Also, don't blame her or agree if she blames herself. What happened to her was not her fault.

- Even if you believe she made poor decisions, remember that no one ever deserves to be raped.

Team 1

Help Her Regain Control

- This may sound weird, but it is very important: encourage her to make small decisions, especially if she is coming to you just after she has been raped. While you are talking with her, patiently try to get her to decide a few small things—whether you talk in your room or her room, whether you go out to get some dinner or bring it home. Don't overdo it of course and don't be demeaning. But, making these small decisions will help her regain control to make larger decisions later.

- Also, accept her decisions even if you don't agree—this will also help her regain control.

- And be patient, it may take her a long time to make decisions.

- Remember that if you tell others about what happened to her without her permission, this means she has lost even more control. So above all, keep her information confidential.

Team 2

Realize Limitations

- Recovering from rape takes a long, long time. Survivors often remain in the early stages of what is called rape trauma syndrome, for three months. More than one year or many more is common for a more complete recovery, even with counseling.

- Some take years, especially if they can't confide in someone or think that they are not believed.

- Refer the rape survivor to counseling.

- Also, it's usually better not to talk to the survivor about your own feelings, especially if you are angry. We suggest you think about talking to a counselor yourself about how you are dealing with the rape, and about how best to help her.

Part D: Other Ways Men Can Help End Rape

Team 1

Before we take questions from you, we'd like to make a few suggestions about how you can help decrease the incidence of sexual assault beyond helping a survivor. Here are a few ideas for us all to think about.

Communicate During Encounters

If you are with a woman in an intimate situation, we encourage you to communicate openly with her about the physical experiences you are sharing and what each of you wants. Remember that as in all communication, this involves listening and responding appropriately.

Cooperation Does Not Equal Consent

Just because a person is going along with something in a sexual situation doesn't mean they have agreed to do it. They might be overwhelmed by how fast things are moving, or they could just be uncomfortable. The only way to be sure that someone is consenting to a sexual act is to ask. If you are initiating a sexual act, just ask the other person if what you are initiating is OK. It doesn't have to be awkward. You don't need to take out a permission slip and ask her to sign it. However, we do think it is very important to be sure that when we as men are with women in a sexual situation that we talk about it with them and make sure both people agreed to do everything they're doing together. Consent is not the absence of a "no," it's the presence of a "yes."

The Freeze

A woman may freeze up when a man does something to her that she does not want. Some men may think she just needs to be "loosened up." For the woman though, this could be a sign that she is being coerced or forced. If she freezes or tenses up, this is probably a sign that you need to talk more about what is going on.

Stop, Ask, Clarify

Finally, if you are ever in doubt as to whether what you're doing is consensual, remember a simple suggestion: stop, ask her, and clarify what you can share together.

Team 2

Help Change Social Norms

We all hear a lot of things that other men say that either directly or indirectly hurt women. It might be an attitude that puts women down. It might be something obvious, or it could be subtle. We think it is important that when we hear these types of things as bystanders, that we find a way to intervene and talk with other men about how their language can hurt women, even if they didn't intend to. Here are a few examples about times when we think it is important to speak up; we hope you will too.

- **Rape jokes** – Rape jokes are not funny. Maybe you've heard a guy say "that test raped me." No it didn't. Maybe he'll tell a joke where a woman is forced to do something she didn't want to do. What is funny about rape? When someone tells a rape joke, it's like making fun of kids with cancer—it minimizes and makes fun of another person's pain. We encourage you to interrupt them or, at a minimum, don't laugh.

- **Challenge sexist behaviors** – Sometime you might hear a guy who thinks another guy is weak say "Hey, take off your skirt." This is just the kind of sexist attitude that demeans women—that makes being a woman synonymous with weakness and inferiority. We encourage you to resist these kinds of sexist attitudes that demean women, and encourage your friends to resist them too. Also, we encourage you to support a woman's right to say what can and cannot be done to her own body, and support how she wishes to express herself.

- **Condemn abuse of women** – Maybe you've heard a guy talk about how he "gave it to her good" when she was drunk and passed out or didn't otherwise consent. If a man you know brags about forcing himself on a woman, we urge you to condemn the behavior. Other men are probably also uncomfortable with what the guy is saying. We encourage you to be the first one to speak up and condemn his behavior. Others will probably respect you more for it. Above all, please don't laugh or condone the abuse.

- **Educate yourself, support others** – We commend you for coming out tonight to educate yourselves. We urge you to continue the process by talking to women and to other men about this issue, taking advantage of opportunities like this and reading material you may run across. We urge you to support other men who wish to educate themselves as well, and we hope you will encourage others to invite us in to show them our program.

We are now ready for any questions you have.

[Take questions.]

Team 1

Our goal was to inspire you to help end rape and the suffering it causes. We hope you will join us in being part of the solution. We have flyers available with resources that you can give to a friend who has been raped. We will also stay after if you would like to talk to us individually.

Team 2

One final statistic before we leave. In the year 2003, the *National Crime Victimization Survey* found that over 179,000 women survived rape and other forms of sexual assault. If you do the math, that works out to 20women every hour. We've been here for about an hour. If this was an average hour in this country, while we sat here, 20 women had an experience similar to the one you saw on the video.

Team 1

Twenty women have just been sexually assaulted. Twenty women have had an experience similar to the one we showed you on that video. That's 20 best-friends, 20 sisters, 20 daughters, 20 women have just been sexually assaulted.

Team 2

Thank you for coming.

Team 1

Go forth and make a difference.

*Note: The author is deeply grateful to Brad Perry, numerous professional colleagues, and to members of "One in Four" chapters at UVa and several other campuses for contributing excellent ideas for improving this script.

A Training Course
for Peer Educators

This chapter provides a course syllabus and class-by-class instructions for how to teach a three-credit course to train male, sexual-assault peer educators to present *The Men's Program*. The course is divided into 15 weeks worth of material, partitioned into two weekly classes of one hour and 15 minutes each.

It may not be possible for you to implement the entire training program. If this is the case, it is suggested that you use the shorter training program described in Appendix F, or pick and choose exercises from the class in this chapter to meet your needs.

The course described in this chapter provides participants with the necessary theoretical and practical background to be exceptional sexual-assault peer educators. The course content includes team-building, an introduction to *The Men's Program*, gender role socialization, sexual orientation and homophobia issues, rape definitions and causes, communication, alcohol, diversity issues relevant to sexual assault, rape myths, rape trauma syndrome, research knowledge, public speaking, learning to present *The Men's Program*, presenting the program on video-tape, a final exam, and a session to evaluate/plan the next steps. Detailed descriptions for each session are included.

The target population for this training program is college males. Men are the preferred presenters because research supports the assertion that the best way to influence men's attitudes about rape is through an all-male, peer-education program (Earle 1996; Lonsway 1996). It is important to note that a woman can be the instructor for the class and the advisor to the group. If this is the case, it is suggested that at least some class sessions be facilitated by a male presenter to allow for single-sex discussions.

The principal desired outcome of this training program is to bring male peer educators to the point where they can effectively present an all-male, sexual-assault, peer-education program. In order to reach that

Chapter 3

outcome, several goals and corresponding objectives are identified below. Each goal has a one- to three-word theme so that it can be referred to with ease later in this document.

☑ **Goal 1 – Team Building:** Create a cohesive team out of the group of peer educators.

- Objective A – Participants will deal constructively with tension in the group.

- Objective B – Participants will challenge each other's beliefs and assumptions without challenging each other personally.

- Objective C – Participants will develop a sense of camaraderie with their fellow peer educators.

- Objective D – Participants will share information on a deep, personal level during team building exercises and throughout the training class.

☑ **Goal 2 – Underlying Issues:** Participants will understand the precursors to, potential causes of, and integral concepts related to sexual assault.

- Objective A – Participants will be able to define and to describe the relationship between consent and force in sexual situations.

- Objective B – Participants will understand the influence of alcohol on sexual assault.

- Objective C – Participants will be able to define the term "rape myth," will know several examples of rape myths, and will be able to effectively confront statements made by people who believe rape myths.

- Objective D – Participants will understand the relationship between gender-role socialization and sexual assault.

- Objective E – Participants will understand the influence of gender differences in communication style on sexual assault.

☑ **Goal 3 – Sexual-Assault Knowledge:** Bring each participant to a high level of knowledge about the prevalence of sexual assault in the United States, across cultures, and on college campuses.

- Objective A – Participants will know the percentage of women who survive rape or attempted rape before college, during college, and over a lifetime in the United States.

- Objective B – Participants will be able to cite examples of how women who survive rape are treated in other countries.

- Objective C – Participants will know how often a woman is raped in the United States.

- Objective D – Participants will be able to define and to articulate the similarities and the differences between rape and sexual assault.

☑ **Goal 4 – Diversity:** Participants will increase their understanding of issues of diversity, particularly as these issues relate to sexual assault.

- Objective A – Participants will understand the level of rape-myth belief among people from different races and cultures.

- Objective B – Participants will understand the influence of cultural norms that often lead to beliefs about gender roles among people from different races.

- Objective C – Participants will know the statistics of interracial and intraracial rape.

- Objective D – Participants will advocate for the appreciation of diversity and will learn to confront participants who attempt to blame any one racial or ethnic group for the problem of sexual assault.

- Objective E – Participants will understand the diverse experiences and perspectives of their fellow peer educators.

- Objective F – Participants will learn why using a male-on-male rape scenario is appropriate in educating men about sexual assault.

☑ **Goal 5 – Rape Recovery:** Increase each person's knowledge of the immediate, short-term, and long-term effects of sexual assault.

- Objective A – Participants will recognize characteristic behaviors women often exhibit shortly after being raped.

- Objective B – Participants will understand the characteristics of the acute phase of sexual-assault recovery.

- Objective C – Participants will understand the long-term impacts of sexual assault.

☑ **Goal 6 – Empathy:** Participants will increase their understanding of and empathy for rape survivors.

- Objective A – Participants will gain as thorough an understanding as possible for the pain and violation caused when someone is raped.

- Objective B – Participants will report at the end of the semester that they more fully understand that rape is a crime of violence than they did in the beginning.

☑ **Goal 7 – Helping Skills:** Have each participant learn several skills that are likely to help a sexual-assault survivor.

- Objective A – Participants will be able to cite five types of helping behaviors to use when talking with a sexual-assault survivor.

- Objective B – Participants will be able to cite two types of behaviors to avoid when talking with a sexual-assault survivor.

- Objective C – Participants will know of several resources on and off their campus that serve sexual-assault survivors.

- Objective D – Participants will understand their roles as educators and resource persons.

☑ **Goal 8 – Presentation Skills:** Increase each person's confidence in speaking in front of an all-male group.

- Objective A – Each participant will speak articulately and appear comfortable during presentations.

- Objective B – Each participant will improve his public-speaking abilities.

- Objective C – Participants will be aware of typical questions asked by participants who seek to disrupt the program.

- Objective D – Participants will know several techniques and responses to typical disruptive behavior and will effectively handle these responses in role plays.

- Objective E – Participants will be able to present *The Men's Program* with the highest possible degree of passion, skill, and polish.

☑ **Goal 9 – Inspiring Yourself and Others to End Rape:** Inspire participants to actively work to change their own behavior and the behavior of others regarding sexual coercion, sexual assault, and rape.

- ■ Objective A – Participants will discuss their own behavior openly throughout the class, will provide thoughtful and self-reflective insights in their journals, and will discuss how their behavior changes throughout the time they take the class.

- ■ Objective B – Participants will know risk-reduction techniques for women and rape-prevention techniques for men.

- ■ Objective C – Participants will present the program to all-male groups.

☑ **Goal 10 – Research Knowledge:** Help class members to understand important concepts in being able to interpret and to apply research articles and to understand how programs are most effectively evaluated.

- ■ Objective A – Participants will know how to define and to explain statistical concepts, such as correlation, analysis of variance, and statistical significance.

- ■ Objective B – Participants will be able to read a research journal article, grasp its content, and apply it to what they know about sexual-assault prevention.

- ■ Objective C – Participants will understand several ways in which sexual-assault programs are subjected to empirical evaluation and will know the strengths and the weaknesses of each method.

Comprehensive Design for the Course

This chapter outlines a training course for male, sexual-assault peer educators and includes training exercises created by the author, along with exercises contributed by many others either for this class or modified to fit the context of this class by the author. Credit is given within this book in several places. Thanks to all for their contributions.

Enrollment

Because this is a class on how to present an all-male, sexual-assault, peer-education program, course enrollment should be restricted to men. Class members should be recruited by the instructor based on recommendations of administrators who have a high degree of student contact, including but not limited to, administrators in resident life, campus programs, campus athletics, Greek life, and the office of multiethnic student education (see recruitment and selection guide in Chapter 4). Nominations for the class and peer-education group should also be solicited from student groups and organizations on your campus including student council, other sexual assault and health-education groups, and activist organizations such as NOW. Registration should be granted by the instructor only, and each person wishing to enroll should be interviewed by the instructor. It is acceptable for a woman to teach the course, given the resources and interest level on your campus or organization; however, to preserve the all-male dynamic, it is preferable, though not critical, that a man be the primary instructor. Above all, it is more important to make it possible for the program to be presented.

As part of this interview, potential enrollees should be asked to present a rape-definition poster. Presenting a rape-definition poster includes defining sexual assault and rape. The candidate must be able to compare the definitions and state that four out of five rapes are acquaintance rapes. Complete presentation instructions should be provided so that the exercise focuses on assessing presentation skills, rather than on knowledge. The purpose of the presentation should be to assess the person's ability and potential to give an oral presentation—a crucial skill needed for their success in the course. While a range of ability is anticipated among potential enrollees, a minimum level of talent in oral expression should be required to enroll in the class. Potential enrollees should be asked the interview questions on pages 56–57.

The class should be limited to approximately 16 students, to make small group discussion with the entire class possible. This also will allow optimal personal attention in class and will allow the instructor the time to give extensive feedback on assignments, especially on the journals. Throughout the recruitment and selection process, attention should be given to recruiting men from different races and backgrounds to gain a range of diverse experiences and perspectives.

Each unit's curriculum is designed to meet one or more of the previously stated goals and corresponding objectives. In each description that follows, the goal number, the one- to three-word abbreviation for each goal, and relevant objectives (indicated by letter) will be listed. This method of reporting will allow the reader to refer to relevant goals and objectives if desired.

Theoretical and Practical Perspectives on Being a Sexual-Assault Peer Educator

Date _____

Instructor _____

Address _____

_____

_____

Phone # _____ E-mail _____

Teaching Assistant _____

Address _____

_____

_____

Phone # _____ E-mail _____

Assigned Readings

Books

Kilmartin, C. *Sexual Assault in Context*. Holmes Beach, Fla.: Learning Publications, Inc., 2001.

McEvoy, A. W., and J. B. Brookings. *If She is Raped*, 3rd ed. Holmes Beach, Fla.: Learning Publications, Inc., 2001.

Sanday, P. R. A Woman Scorned: Acquaintance Rape on Trial. Berkeley: University of California Press, 1996.

Warshaw, R. *I Never Called It Rape*. New York: Harper Collins, 1994.

Course Packet Containing the Following Articles

Douglas, K. A. et al. "Results from the 1995 National College Health Risk Behavior Survey." *Journal of American College Health* 46 (1997): 55–66.

Foubert, J. D. "The Longitudinal Effects of a Rape-prevention Program on Fraternity Men's Attitudes, Behavioral Intent, and Behavior." *The Journal of American College Health* 48 (2000): 158–63.

Foubert, J. D., and S. L. LaVoy. A qualitative assessment of "The Men's Program:" The Impact of a Rape-prevention Program on Fraternity Men. *NASPA Journal* 38 (2000): 18–30.

Foubert, J. D., and K. A. Marriott. "Effects of a Sexual Assault Peer Education Program on Men's Belief in Rape Myths." *Sex Roles* 36 (1997): 259–68.

Grube, J. W., D. M. Mayton, and S. J. Ball-Rokeach. "Inducing Change in Values, Attitudes, and Behaviors: Belief System Theory and the Method of Value Self-Confrontation." *Journal of Social Issues* 50 (1994): 153–73.

Heppner, M. J. et al. "The Differential Effects of Rape Prevention Programming on Attitudes, Behavior, and Knowledge." *Journal of Counseling Psychology* 42 (1995): 508–18.

Koss, M. "Rape on Campus: Facts and Measures." *Planning for Higher Education* 20 (1992): 21–28.

Koss, M. P., L. Hiese, and N. F. Russo. "The Global Health Burden of Rape." *Psychology of Women Quarterly* 18 (1994): 509–37.

Lonsway, K. A. "Preventing Acquaintance Rape Through Education: What Do We Know?" *Psychology of Women Quarterly* 20 (1996): 229–65.

Malamuth, N. M. "Rape Proclivity Among Males." *Journal of Social Issues* 37, (1981): 138–57.

McIntosh, P. "White Privilege and Male Privilege: A Personal Account of Coming to See Correspondences Through Work in Women's Studies," Working Paper No. 189. Wellesley College. Center for Research on Women, 1988.

Sanday, P. R. "Rape-Prone Versus Rape-Free Campus." *Violence Against Women* 2 (1996): 191–208.

Scarce, M. "Same-Sex Rape of Male College Students." *Journal of American College Health* 45 (1997): 171–73.

Note: Both in compliance with and in the spirit of the Americans With Disabilities Act (ADA), I would like to work with you if you have a disability that is relevant to your work in this course. If you have a documented disability and wish to discuss academic accommodations, please contact me as soon as possible.

Course Goals

This course will provide students with the necessary theoretical and practical background to be exceptional sexual-assault peer educators. The principal desired outcome of this course is to bring male peer educators to the point where they can effectively present an all-male, sexual-assault, peer-education program. In order to reach that outcome, several goals are identified below.

- **Team Building:** Create a cohesive team out of the group of peer educators.

- **Underlying Issues:** Participants will understand the precursors to, potential causes of, and integral concepts related to sexual assault.

- **Sexual-Assault Knowledge:** Bring each participant to a high level of knowledge about the prevalence of sexual assault in the United States, across cultures, and on college campuses.

- **Diversity:** Participants will increase their understanding of the issues of diversity, particularly as these issues relate to sexual assault.

- **Rape Recovery:** Increase each person's knowledge of the immediate, short-term, and long-term process of recovering from sexual assault.

- **Empathy:** Participants will increase their understanding of and empathy for rape survivors.

- **Helping Skills:** Have each participant be fluent with techniques of how to help a sexual-assault survivor.

- **Presentation Skills:** Increase each person's confidence in speaking in front of an all-male group.

- **Inspiration:** Inspire participants to be actively working to change their own behavior and the behavior of others regarding sexual coercion, sexual assault, and rape.

- **Research Knowledge:** Help class members to understand concepts that are necessary to interpret and to apply research articles and to understand how programs are most effectively evaluated.

Course Evaluation

Journals	15%
Interview	5%
Experiential learning project	5%
Practice presentation	5%
Presentation	30%
Final exam	20%
Class participation	20%

Journal grades will be on a pass/fail basis to encourage students to place the heaviest emphasis on writing what is personally meaningful rather than writing to get a grade. The remaining assignments will be graded numerically. Final grades will be determined on the following scale:

90–100%	A
80–89%	B
70–79%	C
60–69%	D
Below 60%	F

Course Outline

- Session 1: Course Overview
  Team Building

- Session 2: Team Building Continued

- Session 3: Show Class *The Men's Program*

- Assigned Reading:
  Chapters 1, 2, and 11 of *I Never Called It Rape* and Chapter 1 of *If She is Raped*.

- Session 4: Continue Discussing *The Men's Program*
  Sex, Power, Violence, and Rape

- Assigned Reading:
  Chapters 13 and 14 of *I Never Called It Rape*

- Session 5: Sexual Assault in Context

- Assigned Readings:
  Chapters 1–3 of *Sexual Assault in Context*

📁 Session 6: The Male Box and White and Male Privilege

📖 Assigned Readings:
Chapter 6 of *I Never Called It Rape*
McIntosh, P. "White Privilege and Male Privilege: A Personal Account of Coming to See Correspondences Through Work in Women's Studies," Working Paper No. 189. Wellesley College. Center for Research on Women, 1988.

📁 Session 7: Consent and Force

📖 Assigned Readings:
Chapter 3 of *I Never Called it Rape*
Chapter 12 of *A Woman Scorned: Acquaintance Rape on Trial*

📁 Session 8: Discussion of Interviews
Legal Definitions and University Policy

📖 Assigned Reading:
Chapter 9 of *I Never Called it Rape*
Assignment Due: Interviews

📁 Session 9: Homophobia and Male-on-Male Rape

📖 Assigned Reading:
Scarce, M. "Same-sex Rape of Male College Students." *Journal of American College Health* 45 (1997): 171–73.

📁 Session 10: Socialization

📖 Assigned Reading:
Chapter 6 of *I Never Called It Rape*
Conclusion of *A Woman Scorned: Acquaintance Rape On Trial*

📁 Session 11: Overview of Statistics, etc.

📖 Assigned Readings:
Douglas, K. A. et al. "Results From the 1995 National College Health Risk Behavior Survey." *Journal of American College Health* 46 (1997): 55–66.
Koss, M. "Rape on Campus: Facts and Measures." *Planning for Higher Education* 20 (1992): 21–28.

📁 Session 12: Sexual Assault and Alcohol

📁 Session 13: Confronting Rape Myths

📖 Assigned Readings:
Malamuth, N. M. "Rape Proclivity Among Males." *Journal of Social Issues* 37 (1981): 138–57.

Chapters 6 and 10 of *A Woman Scorned: Acquaintance Rape On Trial*

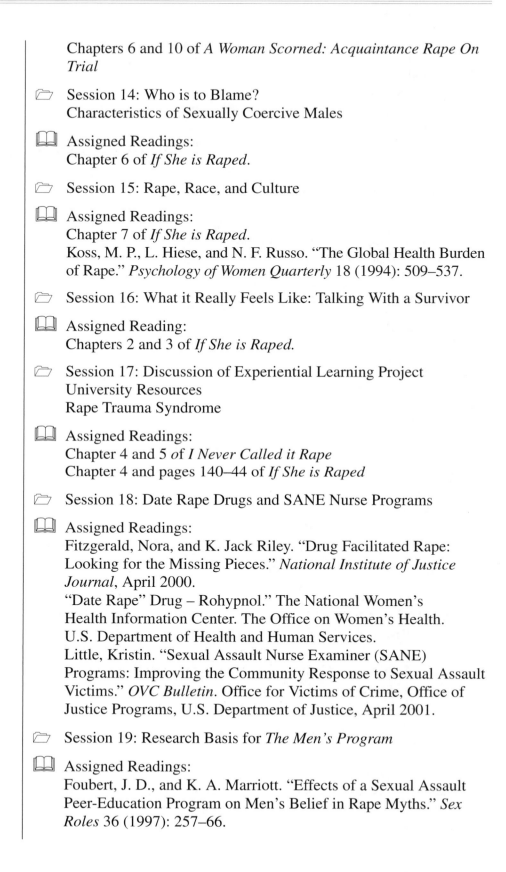

Session 14: Who is to Blame?
Characteristics of Sexually Coercive Males

Assigned Readings:
Chapter 6 of *If She is Raped.*

Session 15: Rape, Race, and Culture

Assigned Readings:
Chapter 7 of *If She is Raped.*
Koss, M. P., L. Hiese, and N. F. Russo. "The Global Health Burden of Rape." *Psychology of Women Quarterly* 18 (1994): 509–537.

Session 16: What it Really Feels Like: Talking With a Survivor

Assigned Reading:
Chapters 2 and 3 of *If She is Raped.*

Session 17: Discussion of Experiential Learning Project
University Resources
Rape Trauma Syndrome

Assigned Readings:
Chapter 4 and 5 *of I Never Called it Rape*
Chapter 4 and pages 140–44 of *If She is Raped*

Session 18: Date Rape Drugs and SANE Nurse Programs

Assigned Readings:
Fitzgerald, Nora, and K. Jack Riley. "Drug Facilitated Rape: Looking for the Missing Pieces." *National Institute of Justice Journal*, April 2000.
"Date Rape" Drug – Rohypnol." The National Women's Health Information Center. The Office on Women's Health. U.S. Department of Health and Human Services.
Little, Kristin. "Sexual Assault Nurse Examiner (SANE) Programs: Improving the Community Response to Sexual Assault Victims." *OVC Bulletin*. Office for Victims of Crime, Office of Justice Programs, U.S. Department of Justice, April 2001.

Session 19: Research Basis for *The Men's Program*

Assigned Readings:
Foubert, J. D., and K. A. Marriott. "Effects of a Sexual Assault Peer-Education Program on Men's Belief in Rape Myths." *Sex Roles* 36 (1997): 257–66.

Foubert, J. D., and S. L. LaVoy. A qualitative assessment of "The Men's Program: The Impact of a Rape Prevention Program on Fraternity Men." *NASPA Journal* 38 (2000): 18–30.

Foubert, J. D. "The Longitudinal Effects of a Rape-Prevention Program on Fraternity Men's Attitudes, Behavioral Intent, and Behavior." *The Journal of American College Health* 48 (2000): 158–63.

Lonsway, K. A. "Preventing Acquaintance Rape Through Education: What Do We Know?" *Psychology of Women Quarterly* 20 (1996): 229–65.

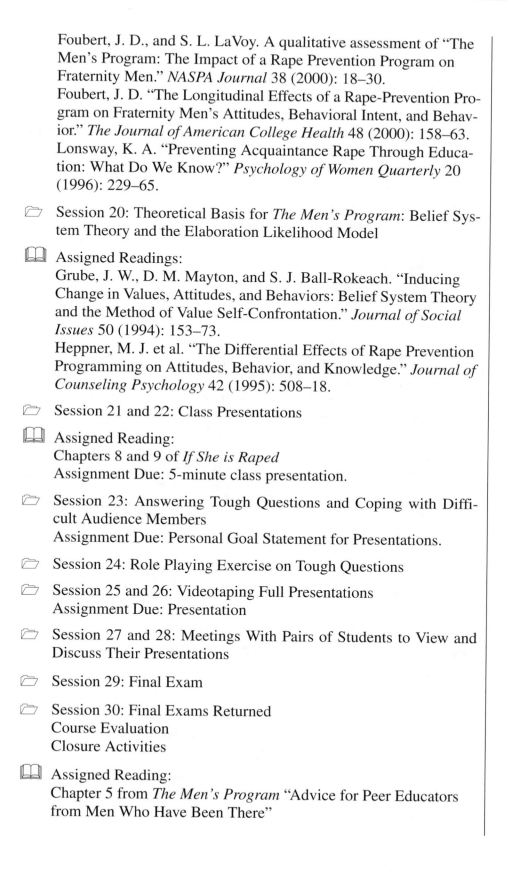

Session 20: Theoretical Basis for *The Men's Program*: Belief System Theory and the Elaboration Likelihood Model

Assigned Readings:

Grube, J. W., D. M. Mayton, and S. J. Ball-Rokeach. "Inducing Change in Values, Attitudes, and Behaviors: Belief System Theory and the Method of Value Self-Confrontation." *Journal of Social Issues* 50 (1994): 153–73.

Heppner, M. J. et al. "The Differential Effects of Rape Prevention Programming on Attitudes, Behavior, and Knowledge." *Journal of Counseling Psychology* 42 (1995): 508–18.

Session 21 and 22: Class Presentations

Assigned Reading:

Chapters 8 and 9 of *If She is Raped*
Assignment Due: 5-minute class presentation.

Session 23: Answering Tough Questions and Coping with Difficult Audience Members
Assignment Due: Personal Goal Statement for Presentations.

Session 24: Role Playing Exercise on Tough Questions

Session 25 and 26: Videotaping Full Presentations
Assignment Due: Presentation

Session 27 and 28: Meetings With Pairs of Students to View and Discuss Their Presentations

Session 29: Final Exam

Session 30: Final Exams Returned
Course Evaluation
Closure Activities

Assigned Reading:

Chapter 5 from *The Men's Program* "Advice for Peer Educators from Men Who Have Been There"

Assignments

Class Participation

Class members are expected to participate fully in every class session. A high amount of class participation is necessary for each member to learn the material and for the group to function most effectively. Class members should not feel compelled to share thoughts and feelings beyond their comfort level. It is hoped that a sense of unity, community, and group cohesion will lead to deep, thoughtful, and enthusiastic participation by all.

Journals

Every Monday, turn in a copy of your personal reflection journal. Journals are shared confidentially with the instructor. Entries should include any thoughts, reflections, and observations you have about class discussions and assignments, such as what we did in class during the previous week, your innermost reflections about the material to the extent you are comfortable sharing, current questions and issues you are struggling with, and anything else you want the instructor to know. Throughout the semester, you might have a variety of emotional responses to the material being presented. Feel free to write these in your journals. Detailed written feedback within your journals will be given to you each Friday. Your journals may be turned in several ways. You can either print them off of a computer, submit them on computer disk, hand write them in a notebook, or e-mail them (if so, be sure to save or print them somewhere). *Due: every Monday.*

Interview

You will have two choices in this class for how to complete the interview assignment. Regardless of which option you choose, in order to be a responsible interviewer, you should give the person(s) you interview a list of campus resources that address the needs of people who have experienced sexual assault.

Choice A

(Note: This choice is based on an assignment suggested by Alan McEvoy, the author of *If She is Raped.)*

If you know a survivor who has already shared her story with you, interview her (emphasizing her complete confidentiality) for this assignment. Alternatively you could write based on a personal experience, or reading the accounts of rape survivors elsewhere. Write a case study similar to those found at the back of *If She is Raped*. Address issues such as the perspectives of victims, their significant others, and others (e.g., law enforcement) implicated in the recovery process. Have them talk about what went right and what went wrong, and then have them make recommendations on what should be done to facilitate recovery.

Choice B

Interview three friends, including at least one woman, one man, and at least one person of a different race from you (these may overlap). Consider having one of these people be a stranger you walk up to on campus. These interviews are intended to include people who do not have any special training or experience in the area of sexual assault. The idea will be to gain increased familiarity with the level of knowledge among people who could potentially see the program, and to gain the perspective of at least one woman about sexual assault issues. Ask the following questions, and any others that seem appropriate. Why does sexual assault happen? Is it anyone's fault? When does a situation become a rape?

For either assignment, turn in a two-page, double-spaced reaction paper to this assignment and prepare to informally discuss what you learned with the rest of the class. If you interview a survivor as part of this assignment, for purposes of class discussion, please share as though it is a fictitious account, in order to protect survivor confidentiality.

Experiential Learning Project

Prior to this class, make an effort to further understand the effects of rape by interviewing a person assigned to you in class (i.e., rape-crisis center counselor, prosecuting attorney, police officer, campus judicial officer, etc.) Write a reaction paper (two pages, double-spaced) based on your interview. In addition, bring a one-page handout for the class describing 1) who you interviewed; 2) their role in dealing with rape cases or issues; 3) a few key points about what you learned from them; and 4) a recommendation for fellow peer educators about whether you believe we should refer people to that individual. These two papers may have similar material. *Due: Session 17.*

Practice Presentation

Present a part (A, B, C, or D) of *The Men's Program* with a partner from the class. Be sure to practice thoroughly, with the goal of not looking at the script while you are speaking (you may have it off to the side to look at while your partner is speaking).

Personal Goal Statement for Presentations

Write a self-evaluation statement of personal goals for improving your presentation style using the handout given to you in class as a model for your paper. Address the feedback you got from the class on your presentation. *Due: Session 23.*

Presentation

Present *The Men's Program* on videotape with another person from class. You will be evaluated individually based on the accuracy and the quality of your presentation. Using the script or note cards is OK, but only for reference. You should not read from the script. This performance should show your best work. *Due: Session 25 or 26.*

Final Exam

During the second-to-last class session, a final exam will be given. This exam will include objective questions that assess knowledge of course content and essay questions that assess the level of which class members are able to integrate and articulate their knowledge of sexual-assault issues. *Given: Session 29.*

Class-by-Class Descriptions

Session 1

☑   **Goal 1** — Team Building: A, C, D; **Goal 4** — Diversity: E

To begin the class, distribute the syllabus and conduct an overview to set the context for the semester. Review some ground rules for the class and discuss class goals.

Ask class members to answer these questions to the extent they are comfortable. To set the context for these questions, say something like this:

"I want you to be able to share why you are here because some people come to this class/training program having had an experience with sexual assault—with themselves or with people close to them— that they want to share up front and let the group know about. For others, they really want to help out but haven't been touched personally by the issue, or wish not to share a personal experience if they've had one.

Whatever your reason for being here, feel free to share on your own comfort level. Secondly, in order to be a strong group we need to determine where our strengths lie. I know it's not comfortable for everyone to say, but please let us know what you do well and how you can contribute best to our group and to each other."

Ask class members to answer these questions, to the extent they are comfortable:

1. What compelled you to take this class?
2. What strengths do you believe you bring to the group?

Session 2

This session will focus on learning to value the experiences of others, increasing knowledge of and sensitivity to fellow group members, and building strong group cohesion.

Praise the members for their willingness to share during the last session. Let them know that today's exercise will be more personal. They can choose to respond to the questions in anyway they wish, including choosing to pass on a question.

Have students divide a piece of paper into four quadrants and write the answers to the following questions on them. Once all four answers have been written, share one answer at a time, around the room, until all answers are given.

1. Where did you spend the happiest week of your life?
2. Where is your favorite place to go when you want to be alone?
3. Who, whether you know them or not, is the person you admire and respect the most?
4. What value is most important to you?

If there is time, have each person say which answer in the group surprised them the most.

Session 3

☑ **Goal 6** — Empathy: B; **Goal 7** — Helping Skills: A, B

🗀 **Week 2, Part 1:**

📖 Assigned Readings:
Chapters 1, 2, and 11 of *I Never Called It Rape*
Chapter 1 of *If She Is Raped*

Show participants *The Men's Program*, presented either by you or by trained peer educators. Ask them if they would take notes only on their thoughts, feelings, reactions, and reflections during the program. After the program concludes, give participants a chance to process their reactions to the program. They probably will not need stimulus questions to do this. In case they do, these should help:

1. When I said this would be a video that depicts a rape situation, did you think a man would be the victim?

2. When did you realize that a man was the victim?

3. How did you react to a man being a victim?

4. When we said that each portion of the program was designed to help you be able to better help a survivor, how did this affect your openness to the program?

5. Now that you've seen the program, what are the major hurdles you think you have to overcome before presenting this program?

Session 4

☑ **Goal 2** — Underlying Issues: A; **Goal 3** — Sexual Assault Knowledge: D

📖 Assigned Reading:
Chapters 13 and 14 of *I Never Called It Rape*

Finish processing *The Men's Program* from the previous class if necessary.

Use Handout #1 to help facilitate this class session, described as follows:

Allow 20 minutes of small group time to discuss the following questions. Allow 40 minutes for the class to come back together as a group to discuss these issues (this may seem like an odd time differential, but experience shows that it works).

Small group discussions (see Handout #1) should focus on these questions:

1. Discuss the relationship between sex, power, and violence. How do we define sex, power, and violence?

2. How does power relate to violence?

3. How does sex relate to power?

4. Is rape an act of power, an act of sex, an act of violence, or some combination of the three? Explain your rationale.

5. What would you say to someone who disagreed with the answer to question number four?

The entire group should then reconvene and discuss what was learned from the activity. One of the main points of this exercise is to see that rape is a violent act that involves sexual behavior. Also, they should begin to develop skills confronting misguided opinions (see question five).

Session 5

☑ **Goal 2** – Underlying Issues: D.

📖 Assigned Readings:
Chapters 1–3 of *Sexual Assault in Context*

Using Handout #19, "Discussion Questions for *Sexual Assault in Context*" by Christopher Kilmartin, introduce class members to gender as a context for thinking about sexual assault. The main discussion questions to use in this class are below. The handout will provide you with thoughts that you can use to guide the discussion and/or share with the class as you see fit.

1. Why is it important to talk about the history of gender and the forces that form gender?
2. What kinds of stories from your own life come up as you think about gender arrangements?
3. What kinds of feelings come up as you think about gender arrangements?
4. How does gender information relate to your own life?
5. What were the gendered arrangements in your parents' generation? How are yours going to be the same? Different?
6. What does all this have to do with sexual assault?

Session 6

📖 Assigned Readings:
Chapter 6 of *I Never Called it Rape*

McIntosh, P. "White Privilege and Male Privilege: A Personal Account of Coming to See Correspondences Through Work in Women's Studies," Working Paper No. 189. Wellesley College. Center for Research on Women, 1988.

To begin this class facilitate the "male box" exercise as described in Handout #26 in Appendix C.

Once you are finished with the male box, ask the class "What are the benefits of resisting the pressures of 'the gender box' for both men and women?"

Next, ask the class to refer to the McIntosh article. Ask them what they thought of it. Use these questions to guide your discussion:

1. Could you see yourselves as having some of the privileges McIntosh identifies?

2. How does this relate to our work in sexual-assault prevention?

Finally, read Handout #16, "Thoughts on Male Privilege for Men to Ponder," to the class. Ask for their reactions to the ideas it suggests.

Session 7

📖 Assigned Readings:
Chapter 3 of *I Never Called it Rape*
Chapter 12 of *A Woman Scorned: Acquaintance Rape on Trial*

Facilitate a group exercise on the issues of consent and force as follows.

1. Tell people we are going to do an exercise to help people understand consent and force.

2. Divide group into groups of about 4 by having them count off 1, 2, 3, 4; 1, 2, 3, 4, etc.

3. Move them into different corners of the room.

4. Tell them that the person in the group with the longest hair will be the leader. The person with the shortest hair will take notes on the discussion.

5. Have each group develop definitions of "consent" and "force."

6. Give them about 10 minutes.

7. Once they are done, have them write the definitions on a chalkboard or newsprint.

8. Compare and discuss the definition—show how they are alike, how they are different, what looks good, what doesn't look quite right?

9. Ask the group the following questions:

    a. How can a man tell when a woman is uncomfortable in an intimate situation? (Refer to "The Freeze" as stated in Part D of *The Men's Program*.)

    b. When is it unclear whether consent exists?

c.   When does sex become forced?

d.   Must the woman say "no" for the act to be rape? (Refer to the video, did the police officer ever say no?)

e.   What can a man do to make sure consent is present?

f.   In Chapter 3 of the Warshaw book, did Donna give Eli consent? Did Eli think he had consent?

g.   What are the benefits of people adopting the practice of affirmative consent as mentioned in Chapter 12 of *A Woman Scorned: Acquaintance Rape on Trail*?

h.   Why might there be resistance to the concept of affirmative consent?

i.   If someone resisted the concept of affirmative consent, what arguments might you use to convince them of its value?

Session 8

📖 Assigned Reading:
Chapter 9 of *I Never Called It Rape*

📄 Assignment Due: Interview

Begin class with a discussion of what they heard from people they interviewed about rape. Process salient issues.

Present your state's legal definitions of sexual assault. Following that, present the policy of your university on sexual assault.

Session 9

☑ **Goal 4** — Diversity: F

📖 Assigned Reading:
Scarce, M. "Same-Sex Rape of Male College Students." *Journal of American College Health* 45 (1997): 171–73.

Facilitate a values-clarification exercise regarding issues of homophobia by using Handout #2.

Next, use the Scarce (1997) article to point out that many male-on-male rapes are committed by heterosexual men, which reinforces rape as a crime of power and violence.

Use Handout #22, "Why Using a Male-on-Male Rape Scenario is Appropriate in Educating Men About Sexual Assault" to guide a discussion on using a male-on-male rape scenario in rape-prevention programming.

End by discussing issues of sexual orientation among women. Process the issue of how some men assume both the heterosexuality of women, and that any woman would enjoy a heterosexual experience under any circumstances. Confront these myths.

Session 10

(Note: Thanks to Brad Perry for contributing elements to this class session.)

☑ **Goal 2** – Underlying Issues: D

📖 Assigned Readings:
Chapter 6 of *I Never Called It Rape*
Conclusion of *A Woman Scorned: Acquaintance Rape On Trial*
Sanday, P. R. "Rape-prone Versus Rape-free Campus Cultures." *Violence Against Women* 2 (1996): 191–208.

Begin class by reading aloud the last paragraph on page 81 of the Warshaw book dealing with how men are taught to rape. Ask the class the following discussion questions.

- In what ways when you were younger, or even now, did you hear these same messages about how we as men should relate to women?

- Were there different messages you received as well?

- How do you think women are socialized about sex?

- How does this differ from the socialization of men?

- How do gender stereotypes about masculinity serve to minimize or excuse sexual assault?

- How do gender stereotypes about femininity serve to minimize or excuse sexual assault?

- Why do you suppose societies that exhibit far more egalitarian gender-roles have a much lower incidence of sexual assault?

Session 11

☑ **Goal 10** — Research Knowledge: A, B, C

📖 Assigned Readings:
Douglas, K. A. et al. "Results From the 1995 National College Health Risk Behavior Survey." *Journal of American College Health* 46 (1997): 55–66.
Koss, M. "Rape on campus: Facts and Measures." *Planning for Higher Education* 20 (1992): 21–28.

In one week from this class period, students will be assigned to read journal articles that may be challenging to read (the two for this class period are rather basic). Lead a discussion about how to read a journal article. Use Handout #3 to guide your discussion. Be sure to discuss what parts of articles will be most useful for them to focus on, how they can best spend their time reading the articles, and some helpful hints on interpreting the information they will be reading. This can be a great opportunity to teach students the value of understanding, interpreting, and applying research to a real-world problem.

After this discussion, talk about the Douglas and Koss articles. Help participants to understand how these studies were done and why these results are so powerful (multi-campus studies with very large samples of students). If there is time, see if they can try to critique these articles.

Session 12

☑   **Goal 2** – Underlying Issues: A, B, E

This class will involve issues of alcohol and sexual assault. For this session, lead students through the following interactive exercises.

Begin by writing/posting the definitions of rape and sexual assault from *The Men's Program* or from a local source and put them on the chalk board or other visible place in the room.

Tell students you will be doing an interactive exercise that will give them a chance to think about their opinions and values with regard to alcohol and sexual assault. Put a masking tape (or imaginary) line in a wide open space. Ask students to stand along that line according to the strength of their opinions where the one side is "Definitely Ethical" and the other side is "Definitely not Ethical." Read the following statements and have students stand on the line according to their opinions. Ask a few people each time why they are standing where they are standing. Bring out main points, note areas in which many in the class disagree. Once finished, discuss the areas in which members of the class disagree as a group. For the purposes of the exercise, "physically intimate" can be defined as touching that is intimate enough that it would be "sexual assault" if consent were not present but that does not involve intercourse.

It is ethical/not ethical to:

1.   Be physically intimate with a woman after she has had two glasses of beer, wine, or two drinks.

2.   Be physically intimate with a woman after she has had six glasses of beer, wine, or six drinks in two hours.

3. Be physically intimate with a woman after you have given, and encouraged her to drink, six glasses of beer, wine, or six drinks in two hours.

4. Be physically intimate with a woman whose breath smells like alcohol but you don't know how much she has had to drink.

5. Be physically intimate with a woman whose breath smells like alcohol, and who has trouble standing on her own, but you don't know how much she has had to drink.

6. Be physically intimate with a woman after she has had six drinks, has kissed you, stops kissing you, and remains still.

    Once you are through, discuss issues where disagreement occurred.

    Next, ask the following questions.

1. When alcohol is involved, when does it become illegal to be physically intimate with a woman?

2. When alcohol is involved, when does it become unethical to be physically intimate with a woman? Is there a difference?

3. What advice would you give to one of your best friends about whether it is ethical to be physically intimate with someone who has consumed alcohol?

4. Does the amount the person has had to drink matter? Why or why not?

5. Does it matter if you are sure or not how much the person has had? Why or why not?

6. Does it matter if you gave it to them and/or encouraged them to drink? Why or why not?

7. Does it matter if the other person kissed you first? Why or why not?

8. How should we as a group respond to questions we might get about whether or not it is OK to be physically intimate with a woman who has been drinking? How about being physically intimate with a woman who is intoxicated?

Session 13

(Note: Thanks to Brad Perry for contributing this class session.)

☑ **Goal 2** – Underlying Issues - C; **Goal 8** – Presentation Skills: A, B, C, D.

📖 Assigned Readings:
Malamuth, N. M. "Rape Proclivity Among Males." *Journal of Social Issues*, 37 (1981): 138–157
Chapters 6 and 10 of *A Woman Scorned: Acquaintance Rape On Trial*

Using Handout #5 as a basis for a mini-lecture, explain the Malamuth article.

Next, introduce class members to the concept of rape myths. To start off, use the discussion questions below. After working through these discussion questions, distribute Handout #6 and Handout #20 to discuss as many myths as you have time for in the class session.

Discussion questions to start:

- What were some of the different prevailing ideas about women and sexuality leading up to the 20th century?

- How were many of these ideas used against women who brought criminal rape charges against men?

- Are these ideas still being used by the defense in rape cases today? Explain.

- How are these ideas/stereotypes about women, sexuality, and rape related to the concept of "rape myths"?

- Can you think of any rape myths that are clearly a manifestation of these ideas?

Distribute Handouts #6 and #20 and discuss.

Session 14

📖 Assigned Reading:
Chapter 6 of *If She Is Raped*.

Have two class members present a short skit entitled *The Legal Bias Against Rape Victims* (see Handout #7). Process the scenario as a large group using Handout #8.

Next, have two men (current peer educators or others as available) lead an exercise in which one role plays the part of a man not likely to rape and one who role plays the part of a man likely to rape. Have role players use Handout #17 to determine what characteristics and behaviors they should portray. Have each role player introduce himself (in character) to the audience and give a speech about his relationships with women and how he thinks men and women should relate to one another.

Allow the role players to engage in dialogue together, confronting each other's beliefs. Then allow the audience to engage in this dialogue. Also, allow the audience to ask the role players questions, which should be answered in character. After the role play is over, give role players a chance to convey their true beliefs, particularly the role player who took the part of the potential rapist.

Session 15

☑ **Goal 1** — Team-building: A, B; **Goal 3** — Sexual Assault Knowledge: B; **Goal 4** — Diversity: A, B, C, D, E

📖 Assigned Readings:
Chapter 7 of *If She Is Raped*
Koss, M. P., L. Hiese, and N. F. Russo. "The Global Health Burden of Rape." *Psychology of Women Quarterly* 18 (1994): 509–37.

Discuss the Koss et al. (1994) article using Handout #4 as a guide. Give a brief overview of the article and lead a discussion on how different countries of the world view male/female relationships and how this relates to the cultural background of people in this country.

Next, divide the class into small groups. Invite experienced facilitators to class (must have diversity facilitation experience, preferable to also have sexual-assault expertise but not required).

Have small groups discuss the questions below. Return for a large group discussion when completed. (Note: These questions were developed by Dr. Sharon Kirkland of the University of Maryland, College Park.)

1. Think of yourself racially, ethnically, and culturally. What messages have you received about your sexuality as a white man, black man, Hispanic/Latino, Native American, or Asian man?

2. What racial/ethnic messages did you receive about the people who commit rape?

3. What racial/ethnic/cultural messages did you receive about those who are victims of rape (gender, race, nationality)? Discuss the value placed on victims and rapists in our society from a cross-cultural perspective (consider race, ethnicity, SES, national origin, religion, education).

4. If you belong to or are affiliated with a particular religious group, what is your religious perspective on rape and sexual assault? If you are not affiliated with a religion, what is your perspective on religion and rape?

After discussing these issues in small groups and as a whole class, discuss where some of the issues that arose in their discussions originated, and focus on separating facts from stereotypes. Find out which parts of the session made class members uncomfortable and why.

Before the class ends, prepare class members for the next session by telling them that a rape survivor will talk to the class. Let them know that you have talked with the survivor in-depth already, and she is willing to answer their questions at the end of her talk. She will be free not to answer a question if she wants and what she says must remain in strict confidence among class members.

Session 16

☑ **Goal 3** — Sexual Assault Knowledge: A, C; **Goal 5** — Rape Recovery: A, B, C; **Goal 6** — Empathy: A, B; **Goal 7** — Helping Skills: C, D

📖 Assigned Reading:
Chapter 2 and 3 of *If She Is Raped*.

Invite a rape survivor to class to tell her story. Pay close attention to issues of confidentiality. Set the proper tone in the beginning of class. If the survivor feels comfortable taking questions, set the proper tone for this discussion.

Session 17

📖 Assigned Readings:
Chapters 4 and 5 of *I Never Called It Rape*
Chapters 4 and pages 109–13 of *If She Is Raped*

📄 Assignment Due: Experiential learning project.

Give students the opportunity to share what they learned in their assignment. Process salient issues.

Next, use Handout #10 to teach the class about rape-trauma syndrome. As you go through this handout, use the experience of the survivor who came into class earlier in the semester to exemplify different stages of rape-trauma syndrome.

After explaining the handout, divide the class into four groups. Each group must help the rest of the class learn about a particular stage of rape-trauma syndrome. Assign each group a stage at random. Next, have each group develop a one- or two-paragraph narrative statement that a rape survivor might say in that stage of rape-trauma syndrome.

Next, have each group read its narrative statement to the class. End by discussing what people learned from this exercise. (Note: Credit is given to James Kohl for creating this exercise.)

Session 18

☑ **Goal 5** — Rape Recovery: C; **Goal 7** — Helping Skills: C

📖 Assigned Reading:
Fitzgerald, Nora, and K. Jack Riley. "Drug Facilitated Rape: Looking for the Missing Pieces." *National Institute of Justice Journal* (April 2000).
www.ncjrs.org/pdffilesl/jr000243c.pdf
"Date Rape" Drug – Rohypnol. The National Women's Health Information Center. The Office on Women's Health. U.S. Department of Health and Human Services.
www.4woman.gov/faq/rohypnol.htm
Little, Kristin (April 2001). Sexual assault nurse examiner (SANE) programs: Improving the community response to sexual assault victims. *OVC Bulletin*. Office for Victims of Crime, Office of Justice Programs, U.S. Department of Justice.
www.ojp.usdoj.gov/ovc/publications/bulletins/sane_4_2001/welcome.html

In this section, teach class members about date-rape drugs and their effects and Sexual Assault Nurse Examiner (SANE) programs. This could be a good session for you to have a SANE nurse in as a guest speaker to address both topics. You might even take your class to a local hospital for presentation by a SANE nurse along with an accompanying tour of the emergency room and examining room areas where rape exams are conducted.

Session 19

☑ **Goal 3** — Sexual-Assault Knowledge: C, D; **Goal 6** — Empathy: B; **Goal 7** — Helping Skills: A, B; **Goal 9** — Inspiration: A, B

📖 Assigned Readings:
Foubert, J. D. The Longitudinal Effects of a Rape-Prevention Program on Fraternity Men's Attitudes, Behavioral Intent, and Behavior. *The Journal of American College Health* 48 (2000): 158–63.
Foubert, J. D., and S. L. LaVoy. A Qualitative Assessment of "The Men's Program:" The Impact of a Rape-prevention Program on Fraternity Men." *NASPA Journal* 38 (2000): 18–30.

Foubert, J. D., and K. A. Marriott. "Effects of a Sexual Assault Peer Education Program on Men's Belief in Rape Myths." *Sex Roles* 36 (1997): 257–66.

Lonsway, K. A. "Preventing Acquaintance Rape Through Education: What Do We Know?" *Psychology of Women Quarterly* 20 (1996): 229–65.

Begin by providing an overview of various approaches to rape-prevention programming by discussing the Lonsway (1996) article. Several key points to emphasize in this discussion are noted in Handout #18. Next, review the basis for and results of *The Men's Program* by discussing the Foubert and Marriott (1997), Foubert (2000), and Foubert and LaVoy (2000) articles with the class. Handouts #12 and #21 will also help you to structure this overview.

Session 20

📖 Assigned Readings:

Grube, J. W., D. M. Mayton, and S. J. Ball-Rokeach. "Inducing Change in Values, Attitudes, and Behaviors: Belief System Theory and the Method of Value Self-Confrontation." *Journal of Social Issues* 50 (1994): 153–73.

Heppner, M. J. et al. "The Differential Effects of Rape Prevention Programming on Attitudes, Behavior, and Knowledge." *Journal of Counseling Psychology* 42 (1995): 508–18.

Using the Grube et al. and Heppner et al. articles, thoroughly review belief-system theory and the elaboration-likelihood model.

Use the following exercises to demonstrate the validity of belief-system theory and the elaboration likelihood model.

Belief-System Theory

After reviewing the Grube et al. article describing belief-system theory, tell class members that you will read two statements, and that you want their reaction to each.

Statement #1:

Too many college students are binge drinkers. You all, because you are college students, are probably binge drinkers. It kills brain cells, so stop your binge drinking.

Ask class members for their reactions. Be sure to point out how belief-system theory states that you must allow people to maintain their existing self-perceptions. If the participants do not consider themselves to be binge drinkers, however that might be defined, they won't hear the message.

Statement # 2:

> *Many of you probably have friends who drink alcohol, and you might drink, too. You might have a friend who drinks too much on a regular basis. If your friend has periods of time when he can't remember what happened, always gets very drunk when he drinks, gets violent with others when he is drunk, and is experiencing academic trouble as a result of his drinking, I have some information you can read so that you can learn how you might help him.*

Discuss reactions to Statement #2. Note the connections to *The Men's Program* (both statements involve helping friends and not blaming the audience for the problem).

The Elaboration-Likelihood Model

After reviewing the Heppner et al. article, read the following statements designed to demonstrate both extremes on the elaboration likelihood continuum:

Statement #1

> *Some water in the United States has polyaceticsorbitol in it. So, don't drink tap water.*

Discuss reactions to Statement #1. Expect participants to say they did not understand it, were not motivated to hear it, and didn't think it was relevant to them.

Statement #2

> *I'd like to share some information about recent tests of the drinking water here at our university. It is important for you to know this because it could impact your health. A virus has been found in the water fountain in the hallway outside our meeting room. It has only been there for a few days. For the time being, please don't drink from that fountain.*

Discuss reactions to Statement #2 compared to Statement #1.

Sessions 21 and 22

☑   **Goal 8** — Presentation Skills: A, B, C, D

📖   Assigned Readings:
Chapters 8 and 9 of *If She Is Raped*

📄   Assignment Due:
Prepare a five-minute presentation of a portion of *The Men's Program.*

Have each person give his presentation for five minutes. Ask the class to write down what they thought was effective about each, and what could have been improved. Conduct a five- to 10-minute feedback session after each man's presentation in which class members give positive feedback and constructive criticism to the presenter. Using this as a framework for your discussion, brainstorm characteristics of an effective presenter. Give class members a homework assignment to do a self-evaluation regarding each of these brainstormed characteristics as they write a statement of personal goals for improving their presentation style.

Session 23

📄   Assignment Due:
Personal Goal Statement for Presentations

During this class period, you should prepare students for how to handle difficult questions and audience members, how to respond to questions about *The Men's Program* and all-male, sexual-assault groups in general, and how to respond to specific questions about sexual assault. For this session, use Handout #15 "The More Interesting Responses We Get From Male Audiences," Handout #23 "How to Handle Difficult People and Questions," Handout #24 "Suggested Answers for a Variety of Questions," and Handout #14 "What Every Sexual-Assault Peer Educator Should Know." Take the class members through each handout. Encourage questions throughout. Ask them for alternative ways of answering the questions and/or dealing with the challenges. Ask them for personal experiences of how they may have dealt with questions and/or presenting situations that are similar to this before.

Session 24

Before this class, recruit five volunteers who are not members of the class to act out parts, as described in Handout #11. Meet with them as a group a few days beforehand to go over their roles and make sure they know what to do.

At the beginning of the class session, teach the class members how to set up a room for a presentation by arranging the seating facing the presenters, checking the TV/VCR for a picture, testing the sound from the back of the room, etc.

Then let the scene in Handout #11 play out, assigning members of the class, one by one, to tackle the challenges presented to them by the role players.

Sessions 25, 26, 27, and 28

☑   **Goal 8** — Presentation Skills: A, B, E

Have pairs of peer educators present the program on videotape. Schedule meetings with each pair for the following week to review their performances. During the question-and-answer period of the program, ask each peer educator two questions from Handout #13 during the part of *The Men's Program* where it calls for audience questions.

Meet with each pair of peer educators to review their videotaped performance. Give each peer educator written comments on his performance, his presentation style, his strengths, suggested areas for improvement, and his grade for the assignment.

Session 29

☑   **Goal 2** — Underlying Issues: A, B, C, D, E; **Goal 3** — Sexual Assault Knowledge: A, B, C, D; **Goal 4** — Diversity: A, B, C; **Goal 5** — Rape Recovery: A, B, C; **Goal 7** — Helping Skills: A, B

During this session a final exam, based on Handout #14, should be given. This exam should include objective questions assessing knowledge of course content and essay questions that assess the level to which he is able to integrate and articulate his knowledge of sexual-assault issues.

Session 30

☑   **Goal 1** — Team Building: C; **Goal 9** — Inspiration: A, C

📖   Assigned Reading:
Chapter 5 from *The Men's Program* "Advice for Peer Educators from Men Who Have Been There"

Return final exams and discuss any common gaps in knowledge about sexual assault. It is hoped that class members will have done so well on the final exam, that this will be an empowering exercise. For those who have not done as well, the instructor should give written feedback on the final exam that hopefully would include a strong reinforcement of the strengths that student has brought to the class.

Once written class evaluations have been completed, have an activity to bring closure to the class and conclude with an empowering, motivational message.

Recruiting Men to Be Peer Educators

When recruiting men to be a part of an all-male, sexual-assault, peer-education group, use a personal approach, particularly when creating the group for the first time. The model suggested below has been used successfully. These recruitment strategies are accompanied by some suggestions for how you might interview candidates to be a part of the group.

Step One: Solicit Nominations

Write a letter (sample in Appendix D) to many staff members on your campus who have contact with students. Include residence-life staff, health-center staff, athletic coaches, student union and campus-program staff, career-center staff, multicultural center staff, select faculty, etc. Also solicit nominations from students groups and organizations on your campus including student council, other sexual-assault and health education groups, and activist organizations such as NOW. Let them know that you are organizing a new all-male, sexual-assault, peer-education group and that you are inviting them to nominate students who might qualify as peer educators.

Step Two: Reach Out to Nominees

Call, visit in person, or send a letter (samples in Appendix D) to every student nominated to be in your group. If you call or visit, tell each of them that you are forming an all-male, peer-education group that will speak to groups of men about how to help a sexual-assault survivor. Tell each nominee that this group is different from other sexual-assault, peer-education groups in that it will focus on identifying positive roles for men to play in helping women to recover from a rape experience. Let each man know that as he teaches men about rape by showing them how to help survivors, his presentation will deal with issues similar to those of other rape-prevention programs, but in a way that makes men much less defensive. Let the nominee know that the program he would be learning to present has been shown to work longer than any other program evaluated in the research literature today.

Tell each man who the person was that nominated him for membership, the specifics of the recommendation and that you are very interested in talking to him further about interviewing for the group. Give him a chance to ask questions. Then, if he says yes, go on to step 3.

Step Three: Schedule an Interview

If the man is interested, set up a 30-minute interview with him. Tell him that as a part of the interview he will be asked to give a very brief presentation, one that will be sent to him (see Appendix D). He will present a rape-definition poster to you.

Step Four: Conduct the Interview

Explain why the group is being formed, what training will take place, and the time commitment involved. This information should have been shared with the candidate when you called, but you can present it in a little more detail. Ask if he has any questions, and whether he is still interested. If so, ask him these questions (for suggested evaluation criteria and a suggested evaluation scale, see Appendix D):

- Given what I've told you about the group, would you be able to commit to it?

- Why are you interested in being part of this group?

- What experiences have you had that would help you be successful in this group?

- This next question is more conceptual (pause to allow him to shift mental gears). Why do you think sexual assault happens?

- Is rape anyone's fault?

- What makes a situation constitute a rape?

- What if you've presented a program, and some guy in the back says something like "All this stuff has been interesting, but what if she gets you so excited that you just can't stop from having sex, and you go ahead and do it anyway?" How would you respond?

- How often do you think women falsely report rape?

- Are there any conditions in which you think women are more or less responsible for being raped?

- Why should we admit you to the group?

- It will be important for members of this new group to be role models for other men in what they say and in what they do—particularly with regard to their interactions with women. Talk to me or us about how you would feel being in the spotlight as a role model on these issues. How comfortable would you be? Why do you feel this way?

Step Five: Decide Whether or Not to Admit Him

The idea for the preceding questions is not to test the interviewee's knowledge (you haven't trained him yet), but rather to probe his general opinions, teachability, and attitudes toward rape. If he states things that cause you concern, particularly if he does not indicate an openness to learn, you may not want to admit him. In my experience, most men who interview for such groups are open and should be admitted, if there is room in your group.

Advice for Peer Educators from Men Who Have Been There

Advice from a Man Who Walked the Walk by Steve McAllister

"What business does a man have working with sexual assault?" Although the dominant attitude of our culture still remains that sexual assault is a women's issue, I am one of a growing number of men who are joining women in the struggle to end men's violence against women. For the past three years I have worked as a sexual aggression peer advocate and educator at Central Michigan University. As a founding member of "One in Four" at CMU I have had the opportunity to present "The Men's Program" to thousands of men, including college athletes, fraternity members, and 4,000 midshipmen at the U.S. Naval Academy. My journey as a man working with this issue has not been an easy one, but it has been the most rewarding ride of my life.

I was always active on my campus, but it wasn't until the summer before my senior year that I became involved with sexual-assault education. I was asked by a friend to join the cast of a program that introduced new students to sexual aggression on campus. The program, designed by Steve Thompson, coordinator of Sexual Assault Services at CMU, consisted of a series of skits that involved domestic violence, stalking, harassment, and sexual-assault situations. I accepted the offer, not knowing that this decision would change my life. What I thought would be something to occupy my summer changed the moment that I met Steve Thompson. I didn't understand the importance of men working against sexual assault until I heard Steve speak with unparalleled passion about how imperative men's involvement in the movement really is. Before I met Steve, my attitude towards rape was similar to that of the men I've encountered throughout my life—I knew it was wrong, and I wished it wouldn't happen, but I didn't think there was anything I could do to stop it beyond not sexually assaulting someone myself. The only education I had received was directed towards women warning them to walk in groups and to stay out of dark, isolated places.

What did that have to do with me? I couldn't relate to their message. Steve showed me that there was a place for men in this movement, and I was determined to do something with the knowledge he gave me.

I approached Steve with the idea about forming a group on campus that educated men about sexual assault. He agreed that there was a need for peer education for men, and he invited me to attend a conference to explore the different male education groups that were already established around the country. Out of all of the sessions dealing with male education, the performance by "One in Four" from the University of Virginia sparked the most interest. They were doing exactly what I wanted to do on my campus: male students educating other male students about sexual assault and how it affects their lives. So, upon my return to campus, I immediately began recruiting men to join our group, and, in November 1999, nine men became the founding members of "One in Four" at CMU.

Although the majority of the responses to our group have been overwhelmingly positive, there have been some negative reactions to our existence. The most significant opposition has come from women who believe that our work actually "hurts" the movement. They believe that the idea that women cannot stop sexual assault on their own, and that they need help from men, is perpetuating the idea that men are superior to women, thus perpetuating violence against women. At first, when confronted with this view I was outraged. I thought to myself, "women complain that there aren't any good men out there, and when a group of good men offer to help end violence against women, we are scrutinized and our motives are questioned." After speaking with many different people, and hearing many different opinions, one idea helped me understand this point of view. A fellow "One in Four" member, Pat, said to me, "If a group of people are oppressed by another group of people for hundreds of years, and all of a sudden members of the oppressing group offer to help them, it's reasonable to think they would question their motives." It took a while, but I've grown to accept the fact that this statement is very true. There are always going to be people who question the motives of a man working with this issue. I've heard things like, "They're just trying to get in good favor with women," or even, "He must have a guilty conscience about what he's done in the past and he's trying to make up for it." The conclusion I've come to after facing these oppositions is that I know, in my heart, that I am doing this work for the right reasons. I am completely sincere in my motives, and I believe that the vast majority of men who work in this field are also. I also believe that if your motives are sincere, it will show, and those who question them will come around, which is exactly what happened with the women who opposed our group. They are still skeptical about whether our program is effective, but they concede that our motives and intentions are completely sincere, and I can live with that.

As I stated previously, the positive responses to our group have far outweighed the negative, especially from men. It is always surprising to people when I tell them that the men on our campus have reacted so well to our program. Instead of the defensive reactions I anticipated, men have thanked us for preparing them for the task of helping a loved one who is sexually assaulted. They have shared with us their fear of having someone close to them raped, and they have shared the regret they feel about not being able to help someone who has already been assaulted. I have had a grown man in full military dress uniform cry on my shoulder because his girlfriend had been raped and he didn't know what to do. The most important lesson that I have learned from presenting "The Men's Program" is that there are men out there that care about this issue, and that want to help stop sexual assault from happening, but they don't know what to do. That, I feel is our job. We give men the tools they need and empower them to make a difference.

Members of our group at CMU believe in the involvement of men so strongly that during the summer of 2001, four of our members, Pat Hanlin, Joe McCarthy, Michael Charbonneau, and I decided to take our message to a national level. With the support of hundreds of people, we walked across the United States to raise awareness about sexual assault (yes, we *walked* the whole way). The trip took five months. Our philosophy was that when people saw four men walking through their town wearing backpacks and pushing a large baby stroller, they were going to ask us what we were doing. It was a great conversation starter, and more importantly, it opened the door to discussion about sexual assault. Not only did we have great conversations with individuals that approached us on the street, we were also fortunate enough to do numerous newspaper, television, and radio interviews. We will never know how many people our message reached, but we do know that our walk brought hope to some.

It's inevitable that when you work with the issue of sexual assault, survivors will share their stories with you. We knew this before we embarked on the walk because we had already worked as educators and advocates on our campus for two years. What we weren't ready for was the number of people we encountered who would open up to us. At first it seemed strange that complete strangers would tell us something that they wouldn't tell their closest friends, but, after thinking about it, we realized that they were telling us because they knew we cared, and they knew we would believe them. We would literally be in and out of their lives within a few hours, but by the time we were leaving they would tell us about how much hope our walk had given them. That gave us a greater sense of accomplishment than walking from San Francisco to Washington D.C. ever could, but it was bittersweet. Why did these people have to wait for us to come into their lives to feel hope? Why couldn't their loved ones, friends, and community members give them that hope? There is no reason that a woman who was raped 15 years ago should have to wait for a chance meeting with a stranger at her place of employment to feel hope. Yet, this was the case over and over again. That is what we have to change.

I have three pieces of advice to any man preparing to start a "One in Four" group or preparing to present *The Men's Program*. First, be inclusive. Reach out to the rape crisis centers, women's shelters, and other resources that are available for survivors of sexual assault. Let them know about your intentions to start the group, and ask them for any advice or other help they can give you. Not only can they help educate you more about sexual assault, you can also meet the people on the other end of the crisis line that you will be referring people to. Second, be open-minded. I learned a lot from the women's group that challenged our group. I wouldn't have learned nearly as much from them if I had not tried to understand their point of view, and we would have probably lost the positive allies that they presently are to our group. Third, and finally, practice what you teach others. Members of "One in Four" at CMU are in a fishbowl, and those who do not necessarily share in our philosophy about sexual assault are looking for any reason to destroy our credibility. *The Men's Program* does not work if the presenters of the program do not lead by example. If a man who was in the audience when I presented *The Men's Program* hears me make a sexist comment or tell a rape joke, the effect is gone. Like Ghandi said, "You have to be the change you want to see."

As I prepare for my fourth year working with "One in Four" at CMU, I am excited to see what the future holds for men becoming involved with sexual-assault education and prevention. There is an untapped resource of young men with passion and enthusiasm who want to change the world. I believe they are a missing piece of the puzzle of ending men's violence against women. It's a daunting task to get them to join the struggle against sexual aggression, but I'm up for that challenge. Hopefully, by the time you are done reading this book, you will be, too.

Finding a Cause by Ben Jamieson

Rape was never my cause. In fact, I was never even a cause person. I went to a pretty liberal, activist high school, and was surrounded by people who were saving the environment, saving the animals, and freeing Tibet. My next door neighbor during my final year of college was like that, too; the door of his room was an ever-changing montage of flyers and posters for roundtable discussions about race and gender, announcements about service projects, and calls to action in response to various worldwide human atrocities. I seem to be surrounded by "cause people." But I have never been drawn in. For some reason I never found an issue that interested me enough to fight for.

To be perfectly frank, rape was an issue that I intentionally avoided. Mine was what I imagine to be the typical male response: it's a women's issue, and I don't know anything about it, so I couldn't really be helpful anyway. I think this type of response is generally motivated by ignorance and no small amount of fear. I was certainly guilty.

As I'm sure many of you understand, I was unimpressed with, and in fact generally insulted by, most—no, all—of the rape-education and prevention programs I had seen. This was for one important reason: they didn't seem relevant to my life. This sounds callous, because of course rape affects people who aren't victims of it, but that's not what I mean. Rape-education programs seemed to assume that their audiences consisted exclusively of rapists or would-be rapists.

Female presenter: "We're coming to you, untrustworthy and vile men, to tell you why rape is bad, and why you should never, ever do such a horrible thing. We know that you are naturally inclined towards it, and this is why we, as women, have endeavored to convert you."

This is obviously an exaggeration, but perhaps not such a great one to express the message that many men take away from many rape education programs. But I knew, long before I ever presented *The Men's Program* as a member of "One in Four," that I would never rape a woman. It's just not something I'd ever be capable of doing. These programs seemed to be a total waste of my time.

So I was skeptical going into my first viewing of *The Men's Program*. It was the video that got me. Remember that moment when you realize what's about to happen to the police officer? It was right then that the feeling started to rise up in me. I wasn't going to cry, but it was that intermediate state where you feel like you *could* cry at any second, and for hours later you feel like you *did* cry, even though you're pretty sure you didn't. Know what I mean? That was me for the entire presentation after that moment. The program left me deeply shaken. But not so much so that I couldn't do what I knew I needed to do.

I went up to the guy I saw present it, John Foubert, holding out my sweaty and quivering hand for him to shake, and said two things. I wanted to have the other guys on my floor see this program as soon as possible, and I wanted to be a founding member of UVa's "One in Four" chapter. I could hardly believe what I was saying. Me, present a program about RAPE? What was I getting myself into?

Alone in my room later that night, I reflected on what I had done. I didn't feel like rape prevention was suddenly a cause for which I needed to fight. The program hadn't changed that long-held stubbornness. But then I remembered my experiences with other rape-education programs, and I had it: this program WORKED . . . on ME! It reached something in me. The obstinately disinterested "no-cause person" had been emotionally affected by *The Men's Program*. And if it reached me, that meant it had to be capable of reaching at least some other men.

I relate this long story to allay any fears that you must come to the field of sexual-assault education and prevention as a lifelong passion. Certainly there are people who have dedicated their lives to this work, and I have a deep respect for them. But rape needn't be your lifelong "cause" for you to be an effective educator. I interviewed for "One in Four" at UVa because the program was dramatically effective. Here was a tool that I felt I could use to really communicate with men about rape. They would unmistakably get the message I was attempting to convey. The program is powerful and persuasive. It is engaging. Most audiences are quite literally left in stunned silence after seeing that video. I've seen it happen over and over again, and sometimes I still can't believe it.

Now rape is my cause.

I don't say this because I believe that presenting *The Men's Program* will have the same effect on every peer educator that it had on me. But beware. Displaying yourself to the world as one informed about rape can bring about a change. Hearing countless women's stories, learning about those experiences your friends just couldn't tell you before, realizing that the statistic from which we draw our name is all too accurate—these new experiences have a powerful effect. With the privilege of counting yourself among a very small number of men doing this work comes great responsibility. Be sure that you are ready for it, for now you have the power to change lives. You have the power and the knowledge to make a difference.

Educate Yourself, Support Others

The purpose of a "One in Four" chapter is to talk with men about how they can help women recover from sexual assault or rape. *The Men's Program* is the primary medium through which we do this. But let me ask you a few questions. If a friend of yours approached you for advice—his girlfriend was raped by a friend at a party last weekend, what should he do?—would your first instinct be to switch into presentation mode and read him the "Helping a Survivor" portion of the script from memory? Or would you be able to talk to him like a friend and give him advice that was relevant to his particular situation? If somebody asked you what your school's judicial process was for handling rape charges, would you be able to explain it? What about your state's laws regarding sexual assault and rape? Are you familiar with them? Do you know how your state defines consent? How about a rape exam—do you know what they're like? Have you ever talked to a nurse or doctor who has performed one? Could you explain the process?

I don't ask these questions to challenge you, the reader's, particular knowledge or preparedness. But I do think that members of any sexual-assault education group should ask themselves these questions and be ready to answer them. The training that new members receive on entering the group is only an introduction to the continuous act of learning and the integration of new information. The training coordinator (or vice president for education, or chair for training, or whatever you call that person) of "One in Four" should be one of the most active members of the group; he safeguards the group's effectiveness by making sure that each member is capable of answering difficult questions and engaging in intelligent conversations about rape. Every member is not only a public representative of the group; he is a sexual-assault educator. You never know when that knowledge will come in handy.

For example, little did I know when I was interviewing for my spot as a founding member of "One in Four" at UVa that less than a year later I would be speaking to 120 of the nation's leaders in sexual assault education and survivor advocacy at an international conference in Orlando. Most of these people had spent most of their adult lives involved in this work, and for the most part they knew their stuff backwards and forwards. My co-presenters and I knew that we would be faced with tough and challenging questions, and possibly some criticism. It was essential that all of us were confident in each other's ability to field these questions and speak cogently. I think we did great. And judging from the comments and applause we received after the presentation, so did most of the audience. *The Men's Program* was given resounding support. But support and encouragement will not always be the response you receive from people who see the program.

About a year after we started presenting, we began to hear increasing criticism of our efforts. Some thought that our presentation was ineffective, that as group members we were not as well educated about the issue as we should be, and that we were a total loss. Over time, we had to recognize that however unfounded we believed these criticisms were, they were conceivable opinions. *The Men's Program* had received criticism in the past, and it probably would again. At times the criticism became hard to deal with. At times we felt personally attacked. At times we were. It's difficult, but extremely important, not to be daunted by this kind of criticism. Rape is a divisive issue, people have differing opinions and theories on how to address it. It is also an issue about which people are very passionate. This can lead to vicious and distressing arguments and defensiveness of individual approaches. Even professionals in the field often forget that we all have the same ultimate goal. Being a sexual-assault educator means placing yourself in a community of people whom you must both acknowledge and respect, even if you don't always agree with them. Keeping members informed and knowledgeable ensures that a "One in Four" chapter will be an active, contributing member of this community.

Communicate During Encounters

While I was at UVa we had three peer-education groups that addressed sexual assault, a Sexual Assault Education Office, professional resources in the Dean of Students office, and the Women's Center, and community agencies who worked hard to prevent sexual assault and support its survivors. Our group worked very hard to keep open lines of communication with each of these groups. We learned that you *must* maintain open communication with the various groups on your campus and in your community who are your colleagues on this issue. It is easy to get wrapped up in your own thing and forget that other people are doing this work, too.

One thing we did to facilitate open communication among groups was to form a Sexual Assault Leadership Council (SALC). This council, which included the president and vice president of each student group working on sexual assault, helped us to better coordinate sexual-assault, peer-education efforts and increase communication between groups. With the information sharing and mutual support and knowledge base that the SALC provided, our members participated in workshops together, created flyers and disseminated information in a coordinated fashion, and got to know each other better. We became friends, both personally and institutionally. As you are establishing your "One in Four" chapter, be sure to remember those people. Strike up meaningful and communicative relationships with them early on. Show them the program and tell them how your group intends to operate. Tell them about the research and the theories. But also listen. Listen to their stories, their ideas, their histories, and their problems. Ask them for their thoughts about your intentions and goals. Find out how you can become a part of the larger sexual-assault education community at your school. These people have probably been involved in this work for longer than you have; you can learn a lot from them. We certainly did.

Tough Work

Much of what I've written consists of caution and concern. This is not because my experience with "One in Four" was at all negative or unsatisfying. On the contrary, I feel that I grew as a person and learned a tremendous amount, while making some of the closest friends of my life and having some wonderful, fulfilling experiences. But it was also a difficult journey. I heard stories of unimaginable anguish and pain, so many that I have almost become numb to the next one. I faced ignorance and insensitivity, and had to try to cut through it. I had my ideas and actions questioned, my motives challenged, and my resolve tested. Sexual-assault work is difficult and draining.

But the men of "One in Four" have a particularly trying road to travel in part because we are men. Few people will acknowledge this fact publicly, but there is a stigma against men doing this work. It is simply a reality of our gender that few men are interested in involving themselves in this field, and so those who do engage receive intense scrutiny. Sometimes you may feel like your input isn't appreciated. But don't let that stop you. You have joined "One in Four" because you believe in the power and effectiveness of men educating men about rape. Hold tight to that belief. Make time in your meetings to remind each other of why you are here. Share your frustrations and concerns with each other.

Present the program as much as you can—there is nothing more encouraging than that guy on the swim team who comes up to you on the street after seeing the program and tells you that his girlfriend was raped last week, and that he wouldn't have known what to do if he hadn't seen your presentation. Or the woman who tells you that her boyfriend is gentler and more respectful of her after hearing you talk about communication and consent. Or the stunned silence that pervades a room of rowdy fraternity men after you shut off the video. Get the word out. Make your group's presence known, through e-mail, through fliers, through word of mouth. Wear your group T-shirts around campus so that people will ask you about them—it's an opportunity to talk about the issue. Spread your message; encourage people, especially men, to talk about rape. Organize public discussions. Break the silence. Participate in other sexual-assault and violence-related programming. Be active supporters of other people doing what you do. You can and will make a difference.

Good luck.

Resources for Advisors and Sample "One in Four" Constitution

This chapter will provide you, the advisor of a "One in Four" chapter, with additional ideas and materials to use after you have selected and trained your peer educators. It also provides your new peer-education group with a model constitution for a "One in Four" chapter.

One way to get your chapter off to a great start is to plan a "debut performance" in a popular venue on your campus or other work setting. If at a university, invite faculty, staff, and students—focus on those who are leaders of groups who can preview your program for their organizations. Encourage RA's to come and say to them that if they like the program, you'll come present it to their residents. Encourage fraternity leaders and athletic team captains to come to preview it for their chapters and teams. Encourage women to come to the debut so that they can see what it is that your chapter will be presenting to the men on your campus. If you put a lot of work into publicity, it can really pay off. With some very minor additional effort, you can get a lot of attention and get off to a great start. For example, work with the press office of your university to issue a press release about the debut. That might sound a bit overboard at first, but you'll be surprised at how much response you might get. The first resource in this chapter is a copy of a press release that was given out to local media when the "One in Four" chapter was started at UVa. As a result of this one press release, three area TV networks came to the debut to film the presentation and interview peer educators—a local NBC affiliate and affiliates from NBC and CBS from a nearby city. All three networks aired the story—as their top news story of the evening. Such efforts on your part can help your group get off to a great start, and help give publicity to your institution and to our important cause.

The second resource in this chapter is a sample statement for the president of your chapter to give at the beginning of your presentation.

Chapter 6

It is important for people in your audience to know who your members are, what their mission is, and their desire to present to various groups. It is also important that the audience recognizes their roles as people who can help spread the word of your availability to make presentations. In addition, it is important to note how pleased you are that women are present to see the efforts that you will make usually to all-male audiences.

After your chapter has been around for at least a semester, and you start off a new year, it is time for a retreat to get things off on the right foot. The next resource in this chapter is a sample agenda for such a retreat. The main activity of this retreat is to have the group write its own mission statement. Who are they? What will they be about? How will they accomplish their goals? Suggestions about how to guide this discussion are included in the agenda. Immediately after the agenda is one sample mission statement. It is suggested that you take a look at this and use it as a way to guide the discussion of your peer educators. If they are missing a point you think is important, ask an open-ended question to determine if they think they've left something out (suggest what that might be).

Throughout your efforts to advise your chapter, remember that the strength of your peer educators' commitment to the cause will be strongly affected by the strength of the bonds among members of the group. Work hard to create the most cohesive, open, and vigorous group that you can. Continually push them to grow. Empower them to make changes in their peers, each other, and in themselves.

Sample Press Release for Debut of a "One in Four" Chapter

Contact: (Name and phone number)
For Immediate Release

Male Student Leaders at UVA Unite to Educate Peers About Rape

Charlottesville, Va.—A group of 16 male student leaders at the University of Virginia has founded UVa's first all-male, sexual-assault, peer-education group. Their name, "One in Four," comes from the statistic that one in four college women have survived rape or an attempted rape since their fourteenth birthday. The group seeks to be the *ones who inform* other men how to help these women recover. To accomplish this objective, they will be presenting a powerful, scientifically proven program titled "How to Help a Sexual-Assault Survivor: What Men Can Do" to men in residence halls, athletic teams, fraternities, and other groups of men at UVA throughout the year. Published research on the program has shown a long-term decline in likelihood of raping—longer than any other program evaluated in published research.

"One in Four" will hold two debut performances to kick off their effort. During these performances, they will present their program and take questions. Members of the group and their advisor will be available after the performances for media questions. These performances will be held on Tuesday, February 2 at 7:00 P.M. in the Commonwealth Room of Newcomb Hall and on Thursday, February 4 at 4:00 P.M. in the Dome Room of the Rotunda. A press packet is available.

Sample Statement for "One in Four" President to Make at a Debut Performance Open to Both Men and Women

Welcome! My name is (insert name) and I am president of "One in Four." We are a new all-male, sexual-assault, peer-education group that presents a program called "How to Help a Sexual Assault Survivor: What Men Can Do." We hope to present this program all over campus—in residence halls, to fraternities, sports teams, classes, and to any other group of men who will listen.

As we start off, I'd like to ask the other members of "One in Four" to introduce themselves to you. (Name, major, and two activities).

And as I said, I am (insert name, state major, and two activities).

We are a group that is united, passionately, behind a cause that is very meaningful to all of us—to work toward ending violence against women and all of the suffering it causes. Based on research demonstrating that the best way to educate men about rape is in an all-male environment, we usually present to all-male audiences. However, today we are presenting to both men and women so that everyone at the university can see what it is that we do. We hope that all of you will support us by encouraging people to invite us in to speak to their organizations.

As we present today, we will present as though you are an all-male audience. We want you to see our program in its purest form, so you will know exactly what it is that we do. Thank you all very much for coming. Now, "The Men's Program."

Sample Agenda for a Beginning of the Year Retreat (after your group has been up and running at least one semester)

1. Ice Breaker

    Go around the room and have each member answer the following questions.

    a.   If you could change one thing, *anything*, about "One in Four" what would you change. It could be something about how we relate to one another, what we do as a group, our program, anything at all.

    b.   When you were trained as a member of "One in Four," you were asked why you joined the group. Now that you've been in "One in Four" for a while, what motivates you personally to continue our work in "One in Four"?

2. Team Builder

    Distribute blank sheets of white paper to each person. Give the following instructions:

    Draw your own personal coat of arms. It is up to your creativity and imagination and if applicable, artistic skills, to come up with your personal rendition. The drawing should include symbols, which represent some personal values, how "One in Four" fits into your life, and significant influences in your life.

    Give the group time to finish—about 10 minutes or so.

    Ask each member to share their coat of arms with the group. Give time for people to ask questions about it.

    At the end, ask the group as a whole the following questions:

    ■   Who did you learn the most about?

    ■   What surprised you the most?

    ■   What is the most significant thing you learned about someone else?

3. Old Business

    Discuss any pressing matters in the group that need focused discussion. Try to stay away from things that can be reviewed at an upcoming business meeting and steer toward those issues that require more creativity and processing time.

4. Create and/or revisit a group mission statement (advisor is encouraged to see sample mission statement following this agenda to give you ideas on one way to guide the discussion).

   Get the group started by dividing them into small groups of 3-4 and having them discuss and record their answers to these two questions.

   - Why do we in "One in Four" do what we do?

   - Why is that important?

   Gather the groups together and have them report back. Note similarities and differences.

   Put people back into groups to brainstorm principles they think the group should live by.

   Return to the large group. Write down each brainstormed principle on a chalkboard or newsprint. Gauge which principles resonate the best with the group. When similarly worded principles are written by different small groups, attempt to come up with a consensus wording. If the group seems to be missing a key area, ask them a question to see if they think the missing area is important enough to warrant a guiding principle.

   Note the principles that everyone agrees on. Write and distribute the list to the group at their next meeting for further discussion, consideration, and a consensus decision on adopting the mission statement.

5. Closing Activity

   Ask each group member to share the thing they liked the best about the day and the one way they plan to help make "One in Four," better in the coming year.

Sample Mission Statement for a "One in Four" Chapter

Our primary mission is to end men's sexual violence against women. In order to accomplish this goal, we shall follow these principles:

- To educate men and participate in an outreach that will help break the silence about and end violence against women. We will take an active role in ending rape and encourage others to do the same.

- To use the most effective, research-proven means to accomplish our primary mission, including but not limited to *The Men's Program*. Accordingly, so long as rigorous social scientific research continues to strongly suggest that sexual-assault peer education is most effective in a single-sex environment, we will limit our membership to an all-male group.

- To put the needs of survivors first, by respecting their confidentiality and helping to provide support in any manner that will help them in their recovery.

- To always act in a manner consistent with our teachings and to set an example for all men by treating every woman with respect. We will also reject all forms of discrimination as well as combat attitudes and social norms that lead to sexual violence.

- To respect and support one another, as well as train a diverse and approachable group, in order to reach as much of the university community as possible.

- To participate in a larger community of people working for sexual-assault education and advocacy while supporting and reinforcing its efforts.

We recognize that the mission outlined above will be difficult, but we are dedicated to hastening the arrival of the day when our group is no longer needed.

Sample–"One in Four" Constitution/Bylaws

Adapt these constitution/bylaws to suit the needs of your particular membership and affiliation.

Preamble

We, the members of *One in Four*, do hereby establish this Constitution in order that our purpose be realized to its fullest extent.

Article 1 – Name

The name of the organization shall be *One in Four*, henceforth referred to as *One in Four*.

Article 2 – Purpose

(a) *One in Four* is an all-male, sexual-assault, peer-education group that seeks to educate male undergraduates about rape. The mission of *One in Four* is to be the *ones who inform* men on campus how to help the *one in four* women on campus who survive rape and attempted rape.

(b) *One in Four* understands and is committed to fulfilling its responsibilities for abiding by the policies of (insert name of your institution).

Article 3 – Membership

Section 1. Members

(a) *One in Four* maintains an open membership to all qualified men, regardless of race, color, creed, disability, or sexual orientation.

(b) Members must be selected and approved by *One in Four*.

(c) Active membership shall be limited to undergraduate men enrolled as students at (insert name of institution).

(d) A member maintains active membership if he:

   (i) attends at least 75 percent of regularly scheduled meetings;

   (ii) appears in all performances in which he is scheduled or provides a substitute when he is unable to present;

   (iii) meets all other obligations of the members of *One in Four*.

(e) A two-thirds vote of those eligible may override these restrictions, excuse a previous deficiency, or modify the nature of these requirements.

Section 2. Selection

Selection of new members shall occur in this manner.

(a) The candidate shall be nominated by a current member of "One in Four," or by a faculty or staff member of the university.

(b) The vice president for Member Selection shall have a discussion with each candidate to explain the nature, the purpose, and the commitment required for membership.

(c) Each candidate shall receive materials that describe the group and include the two scripts from which he must choose his presentation for the interview.

(d) Each candidate shall be interviewed jointly by at least two people, the vice president for training and the advisor, or others as assigned. Recommendations for membership shall be made to "One in Four" after those interviews.

(e) Members shall have the opportunity to comment upon individual recommendations, and then membership shall reach a consensus on each recommendation. If a consensus is not possible on any candidate, the matter will be put to a vote of the members eligible to vote. A two-thirds vote is necessary for the question to carry.

(f) Additional stages of the selection process may be added at the discretion of the active members of "One in Four."

Section 3. Expulsion

A member may be expelled from "One in Four" for:

(a) Missing more than 25 percent of the meetings without notifying the president prior to the meeting.

(b) Missing more than 50 percent of the meetings, regardless of the reasons.

(c) Conduct unbefitting a member of "One in Four," including, but not limited to, committing sexual assault, deliberate deception of the group, and/or repeated deficiencies in group performances.

Expulsion shall be by these procedures:

(a) A written request from at least three members and presented to the president.

(b) Written notification from the president to the member in question to be present at the next meeting and be prepared to speak on his own behalf.

(c) A three-fourths vote of the total active membership.

Article 4 – Officers

Section 1. Officers

(a) The elected officers of "One in Four" shall be: President, Vice President for Training, Vice President for Member Selection, Scheduling Coordinator, Publicity Coordinator, and Scribe.

(b) All officers will assume their duties at the next-to-the-last regularly scheduled meeting of "One in Four" in the spring.

Section 2. Removal from Office

Any officer may be removed from office for being in violation of the organization's purpose or its Constitution/Bylaws, in accordance with this process:

(a) A written request by at least three members shall be presented to the president. If the president is the officer in question, the written request shall be presented to the advisor.

(b) Written notice from the president (or advisor, in the case of the president), the officer in question to be present at the next meeting and be prepared to speak on his own behalf.

(c) A three-fourths vote of the total active membership is required to carry his removal from office.

If an officer is removed from office, the membership may request that he also be expelled from the group. This vote may be taken immediately after the vote to remove the officer from office, and requires a three-fourths vote of the total active membership.

Article 5 – Duties of Officers

Section 1. President

The President shall:

(a) Organize and preside at all meetings of "One in Four."

(b) Meet regularly with the advisor and/or co-advisor.

(c) Monitor and guide all organizational activities of each officer, *ad hoc* committee chair and member.

(d) Be the spokesperson for "One in Four."

Section 2. Vice President for Training

The vice president for training shall:

(a) Provide orientation and training each spring for new members of "One in Four." The training shall include the integration of new members with experienced members.

(b) Assist the advisor or co-advisor in the teaching of *The Men's Program*, the three-credit class described in Chapter 3, in any manner agreed upon by the instructor and the vice president for training.

    (i) If the full three-credit course cannot be implemented, the advisor, co-advisor (if applicable) and the vice president for training shall outline a shorter training program deemed to be most critical to presenting *The Men's Program.*

(ii) The advisor, co-advisor, and vice president for training shall mutually agree upon the roles each will play in the training program.

(c) Report on new developments and research that might impact the group's mission.

(d) Provide regular inservice training for all active members.

Section 3. Vice President for Member Selection

The vice president for member selection shall:

(a) Organize and lead the year-round recruitment and the selection of new members, in accordance with Article 3: Membership, Section 2. Selection of this Constitution/Bylaws.

(b) Maintain the list of candidates for membership.

(c) Conduct interviews for the selection meeting in October and November.

(d) Present recommendations for admissions to "One in Four" at the selection meeting in November. Recommendations shall be a consensus of the advisor and vice president for member selection, or other designees.

(e) Conduct follow-up phone calls with all candidates for membership at his earliest convenience.

Section 4. Scheduling Coordinator

The scheduling coordinator shall:

(a) Schedule all events and programs in which "One in Four" shall perform.

(b) Be the contact person for groups and individuals seeking a program by "One in Four."

(c) Keep the group informed about future performance dates.

(d) Ensure that four peer educators are assigned to each performance. A minimum of two peer educators is necessary for each performance.

Section 5. Publicity Coordinator

The publicity coordinator shall:

(a) Keep the campus aware of "One in Four" through such means as, but not limited to, flyers, phone calls, attendance at organizational meetings, and attendance at university-scheduled training sessions.

(b) Create a publicity plan for the year that takes into account the changing student population and special events on campus.

Section 6. Scribe

The scribe shall:

(a) Accurately record the minutes of each meeting.

(b) Keep a master copy of all minutes and provide a copy to each member within three days of each meeting.

(c) Call all members if there is a change in the time or the location of a meeting of "One in Four."

Article 6 – Advisors

Section 1. Advisor

The advisor to "One in Four," which is not an elected position, shall:

(a) Be a full-time faculty, staff member, or graduate student at the university.

(b) Be a male, preferably.

(c) Provide support and guidance to the organization.

(d) Challenge members to carry out the purpose of the organization with dedication.

(e) Attend all group meetings when feasible.

(f) Be responsible for the budget and working it through the proper channels, if necessary.

(g) Serve as parliamentarian at all meetings.

(h) Teach the three-credit course on *The Men's Program*, each spring.

Section 2. Co-advisor

The co-advisor to "One in Four," which is not an elected position, shall:

(a) Be a full-time faculty, staff member, or graduate student at the university.

(b) Perform duties agreed upon by the president, advisor, and co-advisor, which can include, but not be limited to, playing an active role in the selection and training of new members, attending meetings and performances of "One in Four," assisting the officers and providing guidance to the group.

Article 7 – Meetings

Section 1. Meetings

(a) Meetings of "One in Four" shall be conducted weekly, or on some other regular basis, as established by the membership.

(b) All meetings shall follow *Robert's Rules of Order*, unless specifically stated otherwise in this Constitution/Bylaws.

(c) The order of business shall be as follows:

   (i)   Attendance by scribe

   (ii) Approval of minutes of last meeting by the scribe

   (iii) Reports

   - Scribe
   - Vice President/Training
   - Vice President/Member Selection
   - Scheduling Coordinator
   - Publicity Coordinator
   - Co-advisor
   - Advisor
   - President

   (Note: The chair of any *ad hoc* committee will report immediately after to the officer to whom he has been assigned to work.)

   (iv) Unfinished Business

   (v)   New Business

   (vi) Announcements

   (vii) Adjournment

Section 2. Quorum

Fifty-one percent of the membership shall constitute a quorum. A quorum must be present in order to conduct the business of the group. If a quorum is not present, two options exist: Seek enough members to make the quorum, or wait until the next regularly scheduled meeting. The absence of a quorum does not preclude the scheduling coordinator from seeking volunteers for the next performances.

Article 8 – Elections

The election of officers shall take place at the first regularly scheduled meeting in March in this manner:

(a) Nominations come from active members, and members are encouraged to nominate themselves. Only active members may be considered. All nominations must be seconded.

(b) Nominations are considered office by office, beginning with the president and continuing through the officers, as listed in the Constitution/Bylaws.

(c) Elections shall be conducted by the retiring president. If the president is seeking another term, the advisor shall conduct that election. If the advisor is not present, the co-advisor or someone appointed by the president shall conduct the president's election.

(d) Election shall be by consensus. If consensus is not possible, a vote will be taken by a show of hands. A simple majority decides the election. Candidates shall not be present during the discussion to reach consensus.

(e) If more than two persons seek the same office and no one receives more than 50 percent of the vote, run-off elections will be held between the two candidates who received the most votes.

(f) Only active members are entitled to vote.

Article 9 – Amendments

The Constitution/Bylaws of "One in Four" is binding upon its members. Amendments may be made to the document to meet the needs of the membership and the changing nature of the organization. Amendments may be made in this manner:

(a) Amendments may be proposed in writing by any active member of "One in Four" at any meeting under New Business.

(b) The proposed amendment shall be placed on the agenda of the next regularly scheduled meeting, under Unfinished Business.

(c) Amendments require a two-thirds vote for adoption and become effective immediately upon adoption.

Appendices

Appendix A
A Summary of Research on *The Men's Program*

Three research studies that have evaluated the impact of *The Men's Program* will be described in this chapter. The first study, published in *Sex Roles*, showed that the average man who sees *The Men's Program* experiences a more than 50 percent decline in his rape-myth acceptance (Foubert and Marriott 1997) as measured by the Burt Rape Myth Acceptance Scale (Burt 1980). In a two-month follow-up, a 32 percent improvement remained, an improvement that was statistically significant ($p < .001$). The second study showed that *The Men's Program* also brings about a significant seven-month decline in rape-myth acceptance ($p < .001$) and a significant seven-month decline in men's self-reported likelihood of raping ($p < .05$). In fact, 75 percent of the "high-risk" men who indicated some likelihood of raping prior to the program, reported that they were less likely to rape both after seeing the program and seven months later. Thus, three out of four of these high-risk men indicated a lower likelihood of raping after seeing *The Men's Program*. This study also included qualitative analysis of open ended questions, as described later in this chapter. A third study looked at whether *The Men's Program* impacted men's homophobia. Results of this study showed that men's levels of homophobia are not affected. Results from all of these studies are described in this chapter.

The results of study #1 are also published in Foubert, J. D., and K. A. Marriott. Effects of a Sexual-Assault, Peer-Education Program on Men's Belief in Rape Myths. *Sex Roles* 36 (1997): 259-68.

The results of study #2 are published in the three articles listed below.

The first phase (pre and post-test) of this study is published in Foubert, J. D., and M. K. McEwen. An All-male, Rape-Prevention, Peer-Education Program: Decreasing Fraternity Men's Behavioral Intent to Rape. *Journal of College Student Development* 39 (1998): 548-56.

The second phase (including seven-month follow-up post test) of this study is published in Foubert, J. D. "The Longitudinal Effects of a Rape-prevention Program on Fraternity Men's Attitudes, Behavioral Intent, and Behavior." *The Journal of American College Health* 48 (2000): 158-63.

The qualitative analysis of open-ended questions is published in Foubert, J. D., and S. L. LaVoy. "A Qualitative Assessment of 'The Men's Program': The Impact of a Rape Prevention Program on Fraternity Men." *NASPA Journal* 38 (2000): 18-30.

Study #1: The Effects of *The Men's Program* on Rape-Myth Acceptance Over a Two-Month Period

Rape is a pervasive problem on college campuses today, with 27 percent of college women reporting rape or attempted rape since their fourteenth birthday (Koss, Gidycz, and Wisniewski 1987). Lonsway (1996) reviewed the acquaintance-rape programs published during the last 20 years, finding few programs that had been adequately evaluated. She noted that rape-prevention programs tend to be more effective when targeting all-male audiences, yet she noted that most of those programs are unable to produce lasting change, perhaps due to men's perception that the material presented lacked relevance to them.

A comprehensive study by Earle (1996) compared three-program formats: male-only with peer educators using an interactive format, coeducational with professional staff facilitating small group discussion, and coeducational with professional staff in a large group lecture format. When attitudes toward rape and attitudes toward women were assessed, the all-male, peer-education program was the only condition in which a significant post-program improvement in attitudes occurred (see Berkowitz 1994 for a program description).

The most common measure of whether programs are effective in changing attitudes has been to measure agreement with "rape myths." Burt (1980) defined the term "rape myth" as "prejudicial, stereotyped, or false beliefs about rape, rape victims, and rapists." Endorsement of such rape myths (e.g., women falsely report rape to call attention to themselves) is related to men's intent to rape (Breire and Malamuth 1983; Hamilton and Yee 1990; Malamuth 1981).

Key Hypotheses

- The program would lead to decreased rape-myth acceptance.

- Decreased rape-myth acceptance would remain stable approximately two months after the program and be significantly lower than a control group.

Participants

Five fraternity pledge classes at a small private university in the South participated. Three pledge classes ($n = 76$) constituted the experimental group in which the program was presented. Two were assigned to the control condition ($n = 38$) where no program was presented.

Materials

The *Burt Rape Myth Acceptance Scale* (Burt 1980) was used, measuring attitudes toward rape on a scale of 19 (strong disagreement with all rape myths) to 133 (strong agreement with all rape myths). Reliability and validity information are available in the *Sex Roles* article.

Design and Procedure

Experimental group participants completed the questionnaire prior to (pretest), immediately following (post-program test), and approximately two months after (follow-up post-test) seeing *The Men's Program.* The control group completed the questionnaire twice, one month apart. Rape-myth acceptance was analyzed through a repeated measures analysis of variance.

Results

Rape-myth acceptance fell significantly (by more than 50 percent) in the experimental group from the pretest to the post-program test ($p < .001$). Two months later, rape-myth acceptance rose significantly ($p < .05$), relative to the post-program test, but remained significantly lower than the original pretest ($p < .001$). The control group reported the same level of rape-myth belief on the pretest as the experimental group. An unexpected significant decline in rape-myth belief occurred over time for the control group ($p < .05$). This decline is consistent with other findings that untreated subjects may experience a moderate decline in rape-myth acceptance if they are pretested (Fonow, Richardson, and Wemmerus 1992). The immediate effects of the program in the experimental group produced significantly lower rape-myth acceptance than the tests of control groups ($p < .01$ or less). The control group at the follow-up post-test did not differ significantly from the follow-up post-test of program participants.

Limitations

The sample was almost entirely Caucasian. In addition, the time that elapsed between the post-program test and the follow-up post test was two months. The time gap for the control group was one month. Pretested control group subjects experienced a decline in rape-myth belief. This made comparisons difficult. Study #2 corrected this deficiency by using a half-pretested and half-unpretested control group.

Implications

The new method of rape education through learning to help a survivor in an all-male, peer-education format has been shown to offer promise for future programming and research efforts. Program participants experienced significant decrements in rape-myth acceptance that lasted for two months.

Study #2: Long-Term Effects of *The Men's Program* on Men's Rape-Myth Acceptance and Likelihood of Raping

A recent survey of more than 4,600 college students at 136 institutions showed that 20 percent of college women reported being forced to have sexual intercourse during their lifetimes (Douglas et al. 1997). Some initial research has been done to identify successful components of rape-prevention interventions that impact attitudes (Earle 1996; Foubert and Marriott 1997), however, studies that assess the impact of an intervention on long-term rape-myth acceptance and behavioral intent to rape of male participants are lacking (Lonsway 1996).

Malamuth (1981) found that behavioral intent to rape is correlated with sexually-coercive behavior. Changing such behavior represents the ultimate goal in rape-prevention programming (Lonsway 1996). Thus, measuring change in behavioral intent to rape is an appropriate measure of programmatic success.

Key Hypotheses

- Program participants would experience a significant decrement in rape-myth acceptance that would last seven months.

- Program participants would experience a significant decrement in behavioral intent to rape that would last seven months.

Participants

Members of eight fraternities at a large mid-Atlantic public university participated in the present study (n = 195), constituting 76 percent of the total active membership from these fraternity chapters. The pretest to post-test return rate was 97 percent. The pretest to follow-up post-test return rate was 68 percent. Participants were predominantly Caucasian (91 percent) and had a mean age of 20.3.

Materials

The *Burt Rape Myth Acceptance Scale* (Burt 1980), a measure of attitudes toward rape on a scale of 19 (strong disagreement with all rape myths) to 133 (strong agreement with all rape myths), was used to assess attitude change.

The Malamuth (1981) *Likelihood of Raping* item was used, asking men to report "If you could be assured of not being caught or punished, how likely would you be to rape?" on a scale of 1 (not at all likely) to 5 (very likely). This measure was used to assess change in behavioral intent to rape.

On the seven-month, follow-up post-test, participants were asked open-ended questions about whether the program changed their attitudes and/or behavior.

Design and Procedure

Prior to seeing *The Men's Program*, participants completed a survey containing the *Burt Rape Myth Acceptance Scale* and Malamuth's (1981) likelihood of raping measure, along with other items measured as part of a larger study. Immediately following the program and seven months after seeing the program, the survey was re-administered.

Results

Results showed that seeing *The Men's Program* led to significant declines in rape-myth acceptance and likelihood of raping. These declines lasted for seven months.

Rape-myth acceptance scores were improved when pretest scores ($\underline{M}$ = 46.1, $\underline{SD}$ = 15.3) were compared to post-test ($\underline{M}$ = 36.6, $\underline{SD}$ = 14.6) and follow-up post-test scores ($\underline{M}$ = 40.2, $\underline{SD}$ =11.5). The decline in rape-myth acceptance from pretest to post-test was significant ($\underline{p}$ < .001) as was the decline from pretest to follow-up post-test ($\underline{p}$ < .01). The moderate increase in rape-myth acceptance over the seven-month period was not statistically significant, indicating that there was not a significant "rebound" toward pretest levels. Furthermore, when compared to a statistically equivalent control group, pretested and unpretested program participants believed significantly fewer rape myths ($\underline{M}$ = 38.4) seven months after seeing the program, $\underline{F}$ (1, 138) = 9.52, $\underline{p}$ = .001, than did members of a control group ($\underline{M}$ = 44.5; $\underline{SD}$ = 11.9).

Likelihood-of-raping scores were improved when pretest scores ($\underline{M}$ = 1.5, $\underline{SD}$ =1) were compared to post-program scores ($\underline{M}$ = 1.2, $\underline{SD}$ = .7) and follow-up post-test scores ($\underline{M}$ = 1.2, $\underline{SD}$ = .7). This improvement, in the direction of lower likelihood of raping among program participants, was significant for both immediate ($\underline{p}$ < .05) and seven-month ($\underline{p}$ < .05) improvement. Long-term change did not significantly differ from an untreated control group ($\underline{M}$ = 1.3). When those participants who indicated some likelihood of raping prior to seeing the program were examined as a group, 75 percent indicated a lower likelihood of raping after the program concluded.

Of the program participants who completed all the measures throughout the duration of the study, 80 percent responded in writing to the question: "During the last year, did the program impact your attitudes and/or behavior? If so, how?" Responses to this question clustered around six themes. These themes, from most common to least common, were "Yes, the program made me more aware of rape," "Yes, the program increased my sensitivity to rape," "No, I have always been against rape so it didn't change me," "No," "Yes, it made me aware than men can be raped," and "Other responses."

The responses to this question indicated that the program was effective, given that more than half of the respondents stated that the program affected them in the direction of increased awareness and sensitivity toward rape. This is a particularly positive result, given that the program had been presented seven months previously. It was encouraging that when people said the program did not affect them, they didn't indicate a negative reaction to the program itself. In many cases, they indicated that they were already knowledgeable about the subject matter and that the program affirmed their current opinions. Among the "yes" responses, the major relationship among them was awareness—of the rape issue, of the victim's experience, and of the fact that men can be raped. On the whole, it was encouraging that seven months after seeing the program, most participants were able to articulate how the program either changed their attitudes or how it reinforced their established beliefs.

Limitations

The findings of this study can be most confidently generalized to fraternity men, given that they were the population studied. In addition, only 9 percent of the participants in the present study were African-American, Latino, or Asian, with the remaining 91 percent being Caucasian. Thus, these results can be reasonably generalized only to Caucasian students.

Implications

The study shows definitively that *The Men's Program* is an effective means for inducing long-term change in men's rape-myth acceptance. In addition, this study shows that program participants improve in their likelihood of raping in the long-term, with 75 percent of high-risk men reporting lower likelihood of raping after the program. Given the relative lack of means shown to be effective for eliciting this type of change (Lonsway 1996), further study and use of this program is warranted.

Study #3: The Impact of *The Men's Program* on Homophobia among College Men*

The Men's Program combines the efficacy of an all-male, peer-education format (Earle 1996), with an approach to delivering program content that fits a well-tested theoretical model of attitude and behavior change (Petty and Cacioppo 1986), with a powerful empathy inducing stimulus that leads men to consider rape from a personal perspective with themselves as a victim (Ellis, O'Sullivan, and Sowards 1992). The use of empathy in rape-awareness and prevention programs for men is one of the most discussed issues in rape prevention today. This study sought to articulate a rationale for its use, and explore whether using a male-on-male rape scenario has any effect on the homophobia of program participants.

Empathy is a distinct feeling state. It requires participating in the experience of the other, through having a similar experience directly or through imagination. It is the sharing of the experience that permits a sharing of the feelings that emerge in response to the experience. Barring an actual rape experience, there can be no true empathy without walking audience participants through a male rape experience. Seven studies have been published

---

*This study was co-authored with Andrea Perry, Director of Orientation and Judicial Affairs at Johns Hopkins University.

that assess the effects of an empathy-based intervention on men's attitudes toward rape and/or their behavioral intent to rape. Five of these studies (Foubert and Marriott 1997; Foubert and McEwen 1998; Gilbert, Heesacker, and Gannon 1991; Lee 1987; and Schewe and O'Donohue 1993) have assessed the impact of depicting a man as a survivor. Two studies (Berg 1993; Ellis, O'Sullivan, and Sowards 1992) have depicted a woman as a survivor. All five studies depicting a man as a survivor significantly improved men's attitudes toward rape and/or their behavioral intent to rape. In stark contrast, both of the studies evaluating the impact of describing a woman's experience as a survivor increased men's rape-myth acceptance, and in the case of Berg (1993), also increased men's likelihood of sexual aggression.

Others wonder whether describing a male rape capitalizes on homophobic attitudes or fear surrounding male-male sexual contact. Yet there is no research which demonstrates that depictions of male rape *de facto* evokes homophobia. Many people, men and women, heterosexual and homosexual, confuse or combine sex and violence. We cannot refuse to discuss the rape experience, i.e., forced sexual invasion by a more powerful other, because some individuals in an audience may have homophobic misunderstandings about homosexual expression. Some audience members may connect anal penetration with gay sexual expression; some of these audience members may be homophobic. Our challenge is the challenge of all rape educators: to assure that audience members understand rape, anal or vaginal, as an act of violence, not as an expression of sexuality. In fact, discussing a male-on-male rape situation can bring about a teachable moment to not only develop victim empathy, but can also be used to attenuate homophobia.

To help resolve the issue of what effect, if any, *The Men's Program* has on homophobia among audience members, a pre-test, post-test study was done on a sample of college men. Specifically, participants completed a well-validated and reliable scale of homophobia, the Attitudes Toward Gay Men (ATG) Scale. This scale was completed immediately before and immediately after seeing the program.

Method

Participants were 54 male undergraduates at the University of Virginia. Some were members of fraternities who saw *The Men's Program* as one of several options for meeting programming requirements set by the university. Others were men who lived in residence halls who attended the program with their Resident Assistant. The average age of participants was 19.7. The ATG Scale is a sub-scale of the Attitudes Toward Lesbians and Gay Men Scale. The scale boasts a Cronbach's alpha level of .90 and test-retest reliability of .83. The scale's discriminant validity has been shown by studies comparing groups who would have expected to score at the opposite ends of the scale's continuum. Scores on the ATG range from 10 (extremely positive, nonhomophobic attitudes) to 90 (extremely negative, homophobic attitudes). Participants were given the ATG immediately before and immediately after seeing *The Men's Program*. A one-way, within-subjects analysis of variance was then computed to determine whether or not participants' levels of homophobia changed.

Results

Results showed that prior to seeing *The Men's Program*, participants had a mean homophobia level of 48 (SD = 18). Immediately after seeing the program, participants homophobia level fell slightly to 47 (SD = 18). This decline in homophobia from the pre-test to the post-test was not statistically significant (p = .55). The sample in this study was relatively small, yet large enough for a research design with the power of a one-way, within-subjects ANOVA. A multi-campus study with a larger population would increase the confidence in these findings. It was found that *The Men's Program* has no significant impact on homophobia among college men. Thus, while it cannot be stated that the program has the benefit of lowering homophobia at present, there is new evidence to suggest no ill effects of program participation. This combined with other research showing the program's effects on rape-myth acceptance and likelihood of raping develop an even stronger argument for the program's use.

Appendix B
Getting Off the Ground

The next four pages provide you with copies of the material to print on "processing posters" to reinforce each point made by peer educators. It is suggested that you have these printed professionally on large posterboard. Alternatively, you can either hand-write them neatly on posterboard or copy these pages onto slides for an overhead projector. An order form for the video and a sample program advertisement flyer are also included in this Appendix.

Sexual assault — sexual intercourse without consent, forcible sodomy, sexual penetration with an object, intentionally touching an unwilling person's intimate parts, or forcing an unwilling person to touch another's intimate parts. These acts occur by force, threat, surprise, intimidation, or by taking advantage of someone's helplessness or inability to consent.

Rape — sexual intercourse by force or against that persons will, or where the victim is incapable of giving consent given the person's age or temporary or permanent mental or physical incapacity.

Police Officer's Experience	Common Experiences of Women
A Cop Moves a Trash Can	Everyday Situation Turns Bad
"Don't Make a Move"	Overwhelming Fear
Get on Your Knees	Desire to Avoid Violence
Fear of STIs	Fear of STIs and Pregnancy
Humiliating Hospital Visit	Another Painful Process
Did You Fight?	Did You Resist?

How to Help a Survivor

- Medical and safety needs

- No more violence

- Listen

- Believe her

- Help her regain control

- Realize limitations

Other Ways Men Can Help End Rape

- Communicate during encounters
  - Cooperation does not equal consent
  - The Freeze
  - Stop, Ask, Clarify
- Help change social norms
  - Rape jokes
  - Challenge sexist behaviors
  - Condemn abuse of women
  - Educate yourself, support others

Video Order Form

☐ *How to Help a Sexual Assault Survivor: What Men Can Do* $125
   Includes a free copy of *The Police Rape Training Video*

This video is a performance of *The Men's Program* by experienced peer educators. Men who watch the video will learn what rape is, what it might feel like, what women tend to experience before, during and after being raped, how to help a women recover from a rape experience, what they can do to modify their own behavior in their intimate encounters, and will be encouraged to confront their peers when necessary. Thought provoking and provocative, this video is great for use with fraternities, sports teams, men's residence halls, military units, community organizations, high school boys, or any group of men who want to learn how to help women recover from rape. Women looking to present to men who can't find a male presenter could find it useful to show and then take questions or discuss other material. Also a great tool to show women how men can be educated about rape. In addition, it would be very helpful to help train sexual-assault peer educators, or to help a peer-education program get off the ground.

☐ *The Police Rape Training Video* $40
   (No charge if video listed above is ordered).

First available from NO MORE in 2000, and in an earlier version from the Seattle Police Department, this powerful video is a presentation of a police officer talking to new officers about how to handle rape cases. In doing so, Sgt. Ramon shares the story of a male police officer who went about his everyday business and was raped by two men. Afterward, other officers didn't believe it happened as he said it did, couldn't understand why he didn't fight back, and blamed him for what happened. The raped officer struggled with many aspects of rape-trauma syndrome. This video is especially useful for helping men understand what it might feel like to be raped and is necessary for use as part of presenting *The Men's Program*. Great for Universities, the Military, high schools, and community outreach organizations.

Name _____

Address _____

_____

_____

E-mail _____   Phone # _____

Make checks out to: "NO MORE, Inc."
Mail to: John D. Foubert, Ph.D.
P.O. Box 8795, School of Education, Jones 320
Williamsburg, VA 23187-8795
(757)221-2322
nomore@wm.edu

If possible, please send check instead of purchase order. Tapes usually shipped within 10 working days. NO MORE is a 501 (c) 3 registered not-for-profit organization (Tax ID #52-2102794). All proceeds from video sales go directly to support our mission of: "Working toward a day when there is NO MORE rape and NO MORE need for our organization."

Did you know that many women go to their male friends after being sexually assaulted? Come see:

How to Help a Sexual Assault Survivor: What Men Can Do

Learn how to help a woman recover

Learn how you can make a difference

All Men Are Invited
Tuesday night, 7 p.m. in the basement lounge

Sex, Power, and Violence

The person with the birthday closest to July 4 should facilitate the discussion. The person with the smallest pet should take notes on this form and report back to the class.

1. Define the following terms:

    Sex –

    Power –

    Violence –

2. How does power relate to violence?

3. How does sex relate to power?

4. Is rape an act of power, an act of sex, an act of violence, or some combination of the three? Explain your reasoning.

5. What would you say to someone who disagreed with your answer to number four?

Handout #2

Values Continuum for Gay, Lesbian, and Bisexual Issues

Directions: Put sheets of paper along a wall, in order, that say "strongly agree, agree, disagree, strongly disagree." Clear open space.

Read directions to the group: What I'm going to ask you to do is stand in front of the statements that represent your opinions regarding people who are gay, lesbian, and bisexual. We are not trying to change your attitudes and values. Instead we want to bring to your consciousness what those attitudes and values are. There are no "right" or "wrong" answers. The important thing is that you understand what you believe, not what you think you should believe. You might want to ask yourself why you think the way you do.

- I am comfortable when I am with people I know are gay, lesbian, or bisexual.

- I would be comfortable at a party where gays, lesbians, and bisexuals were present.

- I would be comfortable if a gay man, lesbian, or bisexual talked to me about a problem concerning their sexual orientation.

- I would be comfortable confronting jokes made at the expense of gays, lesbians, or bisexuals.

- I would be comfortable discussing a derogatory comment made by another person about gay, lesbian, and bisexual people.

- I would be comfortable if, at a party, I saw two men kissing.

- I would be comfortable if someone who is gay, lesbian, or bisexual asked me out on a date.

Handout #3

Hints for Reading Journal Articles

This handout is designed to assist you in reading journal articles, particularly scientific studies (Foubert and Marriott 1997; Heppner et al. 1995; Malamuth 1981). This handout will summarize some of the basic things for you to keep in mind while reading through the studies mentioned above. I will discuss pertinent issues in the order in which sections of an article flow: abstract, introduction, method, results, discussion.

Abstract

All scientific studies, and most review articles, will begin with an abstract that summarizes the issue in question, the approach to exploring that issue, and pertinent findings. Be sure to read through the abstract to get the main idea of what you will be reading. Yet reading the abstract only gives you a few basics. Be sure to read the remainder of the article.

Introduction

The introduction begins immediately after the abstract and is not commonly labeled "introduction." It's just understood that the first part of the article is an introduction, the purpose of which is to introduce the reader to the topic of the article and provide a thorough exploration of related literature. This review of the literature can be very useful to read, as you will be able to discover much more about the subject of the article than the study itself assesses. Typically, the last 10 years worth of research on the topic of the article is reviewed, along with a few older studies considered classic. The Malamuth (1981) article, for example, is a classic study in the rape-prevention literature.

Method

The method section should tell you several things. (Note: In the Malamuth article, the method section is labeled *Identifying Individuals With a Propensity to Rape*.) The method section should tell you who the participants in the study were, some of their basic characteristics, what the participants did (usually what surveys they filled out), whether the surveys they completed have been shown to consistently measure what they purport to measure (reliability), whether the surveys actually measure what they think they measure and can be generalized (validity), and finally this section should tell you how the study itself was carried out.

Results

The results section should briefly describe what the study found, leaving interpretation and implications for the next section (discussion). There are several statistical concepts and abbreviations you may want to know a bit about before you dive in and read a results section.

Correlation. Many studies describe the degree to which two variables relate to each other. Variables are said to be positively correlated if when one goes up, the other goes up. If when one goes up, the other goes down, they are negatively correlated. Of course, we cannot assume that because two variables are correlated that one *causes* the other to happen. In scientific notation, correlation is represented by the letter "r." It can range from −1 to +1. A correlation near −1 indicates that when one variable goes up, the other goes down. A correlation near 0 means there is no relationship between the two variables. A correlation near +1 means that when one goes up the other goes up. One positive correlation that has been shown in the rape literature is that the more men believe things like "women who wear short skirts deserve to get raped," the more they are likely to report that they would rape a woman if they were assured they would not get caught.

Statistical Significance. Any time a correlation is computed, or just about any other statistic besides means and percentages, we want to know if it is statistically significant. Basically this means, is something happening here or not? Could this result have popped up merely due to chance, or did we really find something? Statistical significance is shown by the letter "p" followed by a "<" or ">" and a decimal. If $p < .05$ or lower (.01, .001), we can assume that results are statistically significant. If p is higher than .05, we assume the results could have popped up due to chance. This number (.05, .01) refers to the probability the results could have occurred due to chance. A .05 indicates a 5 percent probability of chance occurrence, .01 indicates 1 percent probability of chance occurrence. Later this semester, you will learn that *The Men's Program* changes men's attitudes toward rape, with a significance value of .001. This puts the chances that this effect is random at one-tenth of one percent.

Analysis of Variance. Sometimes we want to know if one group is different from another. For example, we might want to know if men who see our program are any different from men who do not. To test this we use a procedure called Analysis of Variance (ANOVA). The purpose of ANOVA is to test for the significance of differences between two or more means (averages). A difference is called "significant" if the probability that the result could have occurred merely due to chance is less than 5 percent. You will know that an ANOVA is being referred to in an article when you see something like this: $£(1, 286) = 13.9$, $\underline{p}. < .01$. The most important number in this long sequence is the last one ".01." This alerts you that the results are significant with a 1 percent chance we're wrong (good enough). You may also see one of two ways of reporting the means (averages) of groups. Either they will use an "M" or an "X."

Discussion

The discussion section tells you in plainer English, what happened. It also tells you how the study relates to other studies, how the study might be applied to the real world, and what future research is possible.

Handout #4

The Global Health Burden of Rape
Summary of Main Points*

- Costa Rica, Ecuador, and Guatemala legally recognize rape only if the woman is considered honest and chaste.

- Courts in Pakistan devalue the testimony of women of "easy virtue." To determine this, they see if her vagina can accommodate two fingers. If this is the case, they assume she has sex habitually and devalue her testimony. (This finding is from a 1990 study.) They also made a law that a woman's testimony in court is worth one-half a man's. Women who do not meet the standard of proof can be jailed for adultery based on their admission of intercourse.

- In Peru, rape penalties decrease with the increasing age of the victim, with virtually no punishment for rape of older women. Girls aged 12 to 16 in Peru who give birth got pregnant 90 percent of the time by rape, most often by a father, stepfather, or other close relative.

- Guatemala, Peru, and Chile have laws that excuse rape of a minor if the man agrees to marry the victim.

- In 1993, the U.N. Commission on Human Rights finally recognized rape as a war crime.

- A nine-month civil war in Bangladesh resulted in 250,000 to 400,000 rapes.

- In WWII, the Japanese forced 100,000 to 200,000 mostly Korean women to be sex slaves for the Japanese Army.

- Two percent of Korean women report rape when it happens to them (compared to 12 percent in the U.S.).

- Among college students, rape and attempted-rape statistics are: Canada - 23 percent, New Zealand - 25 percent, United Kingdom - 19 percent, United States - 28 percent, Korea - 22 percent.

---

*From Koss, M. P., L. Hiese, and N. F. Russo. "The Global Health Burden of Rape." *Psychology of Women Quarterly* 18 (1994): 509–37.

Handout #5

Explaining Malamuth (1981)

When reviewing the Malamuth (1981) article with the class, review the fact that 35 percent of men in the study reported some likelihood of raping. (This is behavioral intent.)

This is measured by the question:

What is the likelihood that you personally would rape if you could be assured of not being caught and punished? Using this scale:

1 — Not at all likely

5 — Very likely

Thirty-five percent of the respondents answered "2" or above (note that 15 percent of respondents wrote "2," 20 percent wrote 3 or above)

Make it clear that these are not men who "say they would rape if they weren't caught" but rather those that indicate likelihood on a five-point scale. Distinguish "would" from "some likelihood."

Likelihood of raping correlates with rape-myth acceptance, acceptance of interpersonal violence against women, and sexual arousal to rape.

Men who score higher on likelihood of raping also are more likely to view rape as sex that women desire. Men who report lower likelihood of raping tend to perceive rape as violence with serious consequences to the victim.

Handout #6

Rape Myths: Who Believes Them?

Who is more likely to believe in rape myths?

- Men are more likely than women to believe rape myths (Lonsway and Fitzgerald 1994).

- Men who have behaved aggressively on dates (Muelenhard and Linton 1987).

- Men who report stronger intent to rape (Malamuth 1981 [and many others]).

- Men who admit to rape (Malamuth 1981).

- People with more traditional attitudes toward women, more traditional sex-role stereotypes, those who more accepting of interpersonal violence (Lonsway and Fitzgerald 1994).

- Women who have not been raped believe more rape myths than rape survivors (Lonsway and Fitzgerald 1994).

- Students earlier in their college career (Lonsway and Fitzgerald 1994).

Are there race or ethnic differences?

In some cases yes, in other cases maybe. Men in the U.S. born outside the country and non-citizens believe more rape myths (Gray, Palileo, and Johnson 1993). Some studies have found that African-Americans believe more rape myths than Caucasians (Lonsway and Fitzgerald 1994); however, several studies have found no difference between these two groups (Gray et al. 1993; Kalof and Wade 1995). Asian-Americans have been shown to have the strongest rape-myth acceptance of any racial group in the U.S. (Mori et al. 1995), followed by Hispanics and Native Americans (Gray et al. 1993).

Handout #7

*The Legal Bias Against Rape Victims**

Imagine how it might sound if a robbery victim were subjected to the kind of cross-examination the rape victim usually must undergo:

Attorney: "Mr. Smith, you were held up at gunpoint on the corner of First and Main?"

Victim: "Yes"

A: "Did you struggle with the robber?"

V: "No."

A: "Why not?"

V: "He was armed."

A: "Then you made a conscious decision to comply with his demands rather than resist?"

V: "Yes."

A: "Did you scream? Cry out?"

V: "No. I was afraid."

A: "I see. Have you ever been held up before?"

V: "No."

A: "Have you ever *given* money away?"

V: "Yes, of course."

A: "And you did so willingly?"

V: "What are you getting at?"

A: "Well let's put it like this, Mr. Smith. You've given money away in the past. In fact, you have quite a reputation for philanthropy. How can we be sure that you weren't *contriving* to have your money taken away from you by force?"

V: "Listen, if I wanted …"

A: "Never mind. What time did this holdup take place, Mr. Smith?"

---

*Reprinted with permission of the *ABA Journal* 61 (April 1975): 464.

V: "About 11:00 P.M."

A: "You were out on the street at 11:00 P.M.? Doing what?"

V: "Just walking."

A: "Just walking? You know that it's dangerous being out on the street late at night. Weren't you aware that you could have been held up?"

V: "I hadn't thought about it."

A: "What were you wearing at the time, Mr. Smith?"

V: "Let's see ... a suit. Yes, a suit."

A: "An *expensive* suit?"

V: "Well—yes. I'm a successful lawyer, you know."

A: "In other words, Mr. Smith, you were walking around the streets late at night in a suit that practically advertised the fact that you might be a good target for some easy money, isn't that so? I mean, if we didn't know better, Mr. Smith, we might even think that you were *asking* for this to happen, mightn't we?"

Handout #8

Points to Emphasize from
The Legal Bias Against Rape Victims

Rape Myths that the Dialogue Confronts:

- If she didn't struggle, it wasn't rape.

- If she went along with it, it wasn't rape.

- If she didn't scream, it wasn't rape.

- If she's had sex before, or has sex frequently, it wasn't rape and/or she deserved it.

- Maybe she really wanted to be raped anyway.

- Women are to blame for being raped if they are in "risky situations."

- Women who wear attractive clothes should expect to be raped.

Using the Dialogue to Answer Difficult Questions

If you, as a peer educator, are ever asked a question along the lines of "Is it really rape if she didn't struggle," or "What if you know she really wants it but is just being a tease," or "She should have known better than to wear what she was wearing given the place she was in," you might recite a shortened version of this dialogue. For example you might say something like this:

"I'd like to answer your question with another question. What if you were wearing a nice suit, were out walking alone at night on your way back from a semiformal and you got held up. The robber had a gun, you thought you might get killed, and you didn't struggle. You were dressed up, so he thought you'd have money on you, in fact he'd seen you giving money to a local homeless shelter before so he assumed you must like giving money away. Is it your fault, then, for being robbed, or were you the victim of a violent crime you did not ask for?"

Handout #9

Experiential Learning Project

There are two things you must turn in for this assignment. First, turn in a one-page (you may use the other side of the page if necessary) fact sheet describing specifically what a rape survivor can expect if they go to the person you interviewed. What can they expect from the office in which that person works. For example, if you interview the Associate Director of Judicial Programs, what happens when a rape survivor reports a rape to the office of judicial programs? What are the rights of the accuser? What are the rights of the accused? How does the incident tend to get resolved? The second thing you must turn in is a reaction paper (at least two pages; double spaced) based on your experience. This may include some of the information from your one-page fact sheet, but it should focus more on your reaction to meeting with this person. Do you think the person would be a good one for a rape survivor to talk to? How did you react to what they told you about the process rape survivors go through in their office? How do you think the process might be improved? What feeling did you get from talking with the person? How did meeting with this person impact your views on rape and the material we have discussed in this class? The instructor will make copies of your fact sheet for the rest of the class and will include it in the manual that will be created (eventually) for the class. The reaction paper is a private document between you and the instructor. *Due: Session 17.*

If two of you are interviewing the same person, you may discuss the interview together after the interview concludes and may ask each other questions about what the person said to fill in the blanks in your mind. Please turn in one fact sheet between the two of you (obviously, you can work on the fact sheet together). Please turn in separate reaction papers that are your own products.

The following people have volunteered to be "interviewees" for this assignment. After we decide who will interview whom, please call no later than (insert deadline here) to set up an appointment. (Adjust this list to suit your available resources.)

Clinical Social Worker, University Health Center. Deals a lot with rape cases. She helped draft the university sexual-assault policy. If a rape survivor goes to the Health Center, they will probably see her. Call (list number here) to make an appointment with her. Note: Be sure to tell the secretary that you are not a client, that you want to meet with her for an hour about a class assignment, and that she has already approved this request.

A Detective with the University Police. She has dealt with several rape cases. She made a special request that you must get the questions you plan to ask her to her at least one week in advance. She can be reached at (list number here).

Assistant States Attorney. This Assistant States Attorney has prosecuted rape cases that involve students here on our campus. He is very interested in our program and is eager to be interviewed. His office is 20 minutes from campus. Despite the drive involved, he seems to be potentially one of the most interesting interviewees. He can be reached at (list number here).

Associate Director of Judicial Programs. He has dealt with countless sexual-assault cases here as a representative for the university. Just call his secretary to make an appointment. He can be reached at (list number here).

Coordinator for Rights and Responsibilities, Department of Resident Life. She is in charge of sexual-assault (and other conduct violation) cases for our Department of Resident Life. Call her secretary to make an appointment. Make sure the secretary knows you are interviewing the coordinator for a class project (not that you're coming in because you have violated a policy). She can be reached at (list number here).

Clinical Psychologist, Counseling Center. She is the Counseling Center's expert on sexual-assault cases. She has lots of experience counseling sexual-assault survivors. Make an appointment with her through the counseling center front desk. Drop by to schedule an appointment, or call (list number here). If you call, be sure to tell the secretary that the psychologist is expecting the call, and that you are not a client.

Community Educator, Local Sexual-Assault Center. She will be able to give you a tour and information about the county sexual-assault center. This center is the primary location to which survivors are taken for medical/counseling attention if they prefer to go off campus. She is in the office Tuesday's and Thursday's. Call her at (list number here).

Handout #10

Rape-Trauma Syndrome*

Rape-trauma syndrome (RTS) is a form of post-traumatic stress disorder (PTSD) that is experienced by survivors of rape and attempted rape. Not all survivors will experience RTS in the same way. Rather, this handout outlines possible reactions.

Stage 1: Acute Disorganization (days to weeks; three months common)

A.   Immediate Reactions

    1.   Shock "Did it really happen?" "Why me?"

    2.   One of two coping styles is usually used

        a.   Controlled — Talks about assault in a flat voice, shows no emotion, numb

        b.   Expressed — Visibly upset, angry, fearful, anxious

B.   Physical Reactions

    1.   Shock — (Unable to concentrate, blood pressure change, rapid pulse)

    2.   Sleeping or eating changes

    3.   Symptoms in the area of the body that was attacked

    4.   Loss of sex drive, other sex disturbances

    5.   Fatigue

C.   Emotional Reactions

    1.   Fear (of retaliation, of meeting the attacker, of being alone, of opinions of others, of dying, of further injury)

    2.   Helplessness, loss of control

    3.   Repression, denial

    4.   Minimizing the incident ("He didn't really hurt me.")

    5.   Shame, self-blame, guilt, humiliation, embarrassment, degradation

    6.   Unwilling to talk about all or part of the incident

    7.   Anger, revenge, retaliation

    8.   Can't cope with own rage and hostility

    9.   Irritation

---

*Adapted with permission from *Rape Trauma Syndrome*. Paper presented at the meeting of Virginians Aligned Against Sexual Assault, November 1992, Richmond, Va.

10. Mood swings, over-reactive

11. Overprotective

12. Depression

13. Lowered self-esteem

14. Anxiety

15. Can't concentrate

16. Can't care for self, perform on job/in school, impacts interpersonal relationships

Stage 2: Denial Phase (one to three months)

A. Avoids Discussion and Thoughts of the Rape

    1. Does not express own anger

    2. Attempts to forget the whole thing

    3. Puts the rape "in the past"

    4. Stops thinking of the assault every day

Stage 3: Long-Term Reorganization (six to 12 Months)

A. Physical Changes

    1. Vaginal problems

    2. Menstrual changes

    3. Headaches, stomach cramps

    4. Eating/sleeping disturbances

    5. Easily startled

B. Psychological Changes

    1. Nightmares about the rape

    2. Flashbacks

    3. Fear of crowds, being alone, sleeping, similar locations to rape scene

    4. Lowered self-esteem

C. Social Changes

    1. Trades freedom for security

    2. Changes daily routine

    3. Stays home more

    4. Drops out of school/work

    5. Changes in frequency of time spent with family

6. Moves, changes jobs, phone number

7. Lack or loss of support from significant others

D. Sexual Changes

   1. Fear of sex

   2. Lack of sexual desire

   3. May greatly increase frequency of having sex

Stage 4: Integration/Recovery (after Reorganization)

A. Resolution

   1. Feels safe and in control

   2. Can trust people again

   3. No longer fearful

   4. Blames the rapist

   5. Pursues legal action

   6. Believes self to be normal

   7. Expresses and resolves anger

   8. Assault becomes integrated into personal history

   9. Compassion and advocacy for survivors

Note: Time frames listed throughout the document are approximate and assume the survivor discusses her or his emotions soon after the assault and receives appropriate support. Without support, several years or decades may pass before the victim recovers.

Handout #11

Dealing With Difficult Audience Members

The scene opens:

John, playing the role of the "scheduling coordinator" for the group meets "RA" David at the door. David and John shake hands, and David then greets the other members of the group.

DAVID: *[after greeting everyone]* I haven't really had time to set up the room yet. You guys will be presenting in there *[point to classroom]. [Group then proceeds to classroom and sets up.]*

DAVID: Actually, the guys on my floor really don't want to come, but I tried hard.

JOHN: I bet we can convince them to come. Lets go guys!

[Group enters fireside lounge. Scott, Mike, Will, and Beth are sitting in different "rooms." Scott's door is knocked on first. {1} Numbers in brackets stand for the number of the peer educator who has to interact with you.]

SCOTT: You say you have too much homework to do, and that you really need to study for a test for next week. *[As they try to convince you to come, be evasive, but get interested when they tell you how the program seeks to be a nonconfrontational approach to educating men about sexual assault. Give in and come to the program.]*

WILL: {2} When they ask you to come, tell them that you don't need a rape program because you're not a rapist. Tell them you find it insulting that they are coming on to the floor to preach about rape when guys on the floor are "cool guys who wouldn't hurt anybody." Tell them they should go over to the "damn frat row" or something and leave your floor alone. *[After they try a few ways to convince you to come, give in and come to the program.]*

MIKE: {3} *[Look very busy trying to set up a party for this weekend. Act like you are talking on a phone with another guy and say]* he should come to your party because there will be a lot of easy girls who will be there and that he's guaranteed to get laid. *[Once they get your attention (make it hard for them) be a little rude to them (not too rude.)]* Finally, when they say that it will only be an hour, and that you might learn how to help a woman recover from a rape experience, say you'll come. *[Make sure they know (by a comment "under your breath") that you're coming so you can learn more about rape so women will be thinking you're more sensitive and you'll be better able to get into their pants.]*

DAVID: {4} Thank the guys for coming and say you're going back to your room to get some work done. *[Start to walk off, until they try to convince you to come to the program.]* When they do, say that you had to do the program for your guys because there was a rape on the floor recently and you don't want to be in the room in case the subject comes up.

You just want to do what you have to (the program) and let the whole thing go away. *[In the end, once they try a few ways to get you to come, give in and come to the program.]*

BETH: {5} *[As the group is starting to leave the room (they will probably ignore you) ask if you can come to the program. When they start to say no, interrupt them. Be visibly angry. Use arguments why you should be able to go such as:]* Why the hell can't I go, you're presenting in my public lounge; why can't women go, this is just one more example of men being sexist and leaving women out of discussions that they should be involved with, after all it is women who are raped. Well I am a rape survivor, and maybe I could teach those guys a thing or two. *[Eventually, accept their arguments only when they say three things: 1) The presence of women increases men's defensiveness; 2) they will let you see the program at another time if you want to in a performance just for women; and 3) make sure they give you a list of resources.]* At the end, thank them for what they are doing and apologize for giving them a hard time. *[You can now leave. Thanks for your help!]*

FOUR GUYS: *[Sit down in chairs near each other. Keep talking among yourselves about one of these two topics:]* 1) Mike's party where all the easy girls are coming; 2) The bitch on the floor who cried rape last week. As the guys try to start the program keep talking until one of them uses an effective method to get your attention. *[Let them work a little bit to get your attention but don't be too rude yet.]* {6}

[The program will "fast forward" to right after the video has finished. The video has described a situation in which two men rape a police officer. A peer educator {7} will read a paragraph that says] "because of our anatomy as men ..." ending with "women have during and after being sexually assaulted."

MIKE: *[After he finishes reading the paragraph say]* What the hell do three fags having sex in an alley have to do with women getting raped? *[Disagree with everything the educator says. Finally, he will try to establish the common ground that rape is bad. Accept this response and stop challenging him, but only when he and you agree that rape is bad — even if you disagree with what rape is.]*

[The program will "fast forward" to a peer educator {8} saying that one in four college women survive rape or attempted rape. He will end by saying] "knowing that, what can we do?"

WILL: *[Jump in after he finishes his line and say]* One in four? That's a buncha of crap. There is no way that 25 percent of girls here have been raped. You really think that there are that many rapists grabbing girls in the parking lots of this campus? It would be in the school newspaper every day? Where did you get that ridiculous idea about 25 percent? You're full of it! *[Accept his answer after he explains that 1) most rapes are acquaintance rapes, not by men who grab women in parking lots and 2) that the 25 percent statistic came from a nationwide survey of 32 colleges.]*

[The program will "fast forward" to a peer educator {9} saying that] he'll make some suggestions as to how you can end rape. Once he finishes saying, "just because she is going

along with something, doesn't mean she has agreed to it. Make sure you know what she has agreed to."

SCOTT: *[Interrupt as soon as he finishes this line]* OK, you said this was a program on how to help a survivor and now you're preaching to us about what you dorks say we should and should not do. What the hell are you talking about this for? *[Give in after they try a few ways to say that they are just giving you some suggestions for you to think about.]*

DAVID: *[Ask]* {10} Fine, but how are we supposed to know if she's agreed to something or not. That stop, ask, clarify stuff is for wimps. If I want it, I'll get it, and that's all there is to it. *[Give in at some point.]*

   [Program then reaches the point where questions are taken.]

MIKE: *[Ask]* {11} Isn't the only reason you're here is because that bitch Beth cried rape last week after she had sex with Bob and then regretted it the next morning?

   [For the following questions, the instructor will choose the peer educator to answer them.]

WILL: OK, I think I'm starting to see your point that rape is a problem, but what about all those men, like Bob, that get falsely accused. No one cares about them. All those men who get falsely accused just get shafted. What about them?

DAVID: I see what you guys are saying, but the guys on my hall are pretty horny. If a woman gets them excited when they're kissing and stuff, and she starts touching him, of course he's going to want to have sex with her and *of course* he can't stop himself. At a certain point, sex is inevitable and it is going to happen.

SCOTT: OK, like what about those girls who wear cut-off jeans, a skin-tight top, high heels, and an attitude. You can't tell me they're not partially responsible for rape then.

MIKE: I've heard that rape is about power and control, not sex. Yeah right. Anyway, what do you think?

WILL: I think rape happens because men and women just don't communicate well and that's all there is to it. You agree don't you?

SCOTT: OK. I think it's total bull that if a woman and a man are both drunk, and they have sex, legally, that's rape. That sucks. Why is it automatically assumed that the man raped the woman. After all, even if she said yes, the law still says its rape. The whole system is set up to screw us men and it sucks. What do you have to say about that?

Handout #12

Research and Theoretical Basis of *The Men's Program*

- One in four college women have experienced rape or attempted rape since their fourteenth birthday.

- Peer-education programs are more effective.

- All-male environments are more successful than mixed environments for changing men.

- Increasing empathy with rape survivors decreases men's likelihood of raping.

- Increasing men's aversion to rape decreases the likelihood they will rape.

- Nine studies have been done on how men are affected by hearing a rape story. Six, which described a male-on-male rape experience, led to decreased rape-myth acceptance and/or likelihood of raping. Three, which described a male-on-female rape experience, actually led to increased rape-myth acceptance and/or likelihood of raping.

- Changing attitudes must occur in a way that people maintain their current values and perceptions of themselves to be lasting (belief-system theory).

- Attitude change is more lasting when people are motivated to hear a message, are able to understand the material, and believe the information being presented is relevant to them (elaboration-likelihood model).

Handout #13

Difficult Questions for Peer Educators

⊠ I think I understood all that stuff you said about helping a survivor, but that video made me angry. I really don't think a cop getting raped by two fags in an alley has anything to do with a situation where a guy gets a little aggressive with a woman because he wants some. Isn't it too big a difference between that cop getting nailed up the butt and an aggressive hookup?

⊠ I think the one-in-four statistic is a bunch of crap. There is no way that one in four girls here have been raped. Do you really think that there are that many rapists grabbing girls in parking lots on this campus? It would be in the school newspaper every day. Where did you get that ridiculous idea about one in four?

⊠ OK, the program was pretty good. But that "stop, ask, clarify" stuff is a bunch of crap. And you want me to be some feminist by resisting sexist attitudes? Yeah, right. Why should I do that crap?

⊠ OK. I think it's total bull that if a woman and a man are both drunk, and they have sex, legally, that's rape. That sucks. Why is it automatically assumed that the man raped the woman. After all, even if she said yes, the law still says it's rape. The whole system is set up to screw us men and it sucks. What do you have to say about that?

⊠ Yeah, but what about all those guys who are falsely accused?

⊠ But what about when a woman gets a guy so excited that he can't stop?

⊠ What about those women who wear clothes that just advertise the fact that they want it. You can't tell me they're not partially responsible for rape then.

⊠ Many say rape is about power and control and not sex, what do you think?

⊠ I think men and women just need to learn to communicate better. Rape wouldn't happen then, would it?

Handout #14

How Often Does Rape Happen to Women?

- One in four college women report surviving rape (15 percent) or attempted rape (12 percent) since their fourteenth birthday. (1)

- In a study by the U.S. Centers for Disease control of 5,000 college students at over 100 colleges, 20 percent of women answered "yes" to the question, "In your lifetime have you been forced to submit to sexual intercourse against your will?" Thus, one in five college women has been raped at some point in her lifetime. (2)

- In a typical academic year, 3 percent of college women report surviving rape or attempted rape. This does not include the summer, when many more rapes occur. (3)

- In the year 2003, 179,000 women survived rape and sexual assault. This computes to 20 women every hour. (4)

- A survey of high school students found that one in five had experienced forced sex (rape). Half of these girls told no one about the incident. (5)

- Rape is common worldwide, with relatively similar rates of incidence across countries, with 19 to 28 percent of college women reporting rape or attempted rape in several countries. In many countries, survivors are treated far worse than in the U.S. (6)

Are Men Raped?

- Three percent of college men report surviving rape or attempted rape as a child or adult. (3)

- In a study by the U.S. Centers for Disease Control of 5,000 college students at over 100 colleges, 4 percent of men answered "yes" to the question "In your lifetime have you been forced to submit to sexual intercourse against your will?" (2)

Who Are the Perpetrators?

- Ninety-nine percent of people who rape are men, 60 percent are Caucasian. (7)

- Between 62 percent (4) and 84 percent (1) of survivors knew their attacker.

- Eight percent of men admit committing acts that meet the legal definition of rape or attempted rape. Of these men who committed rape, 84 percent said that what they did was definitely not rape. (1)

- More than one in five men report "becoming so sexually aroused that they could not stop themselves from having sex, even though the woman did not consent." (8)

- Thirty-five percent of men report at least some degree of likelihood of raping if they could be assured they wouldn't be caught or punished. (9)

- One out of every 500 college students is infected with HIV, the virus that causes AIDS. (10)

- First-year students in college tend to believe more rape myths than seniors. (11)

- Sexual-assault offenders were substantially more likely than any other category of violent criminal to report experiencing physical or sexual abuse as children. (7)

- In one study, 98 percent of men who raped boys reported that they were heterosexual. (12)

Who Are the Survivors?

- Forty-one percent of college women who are raped were virgins at the time. (1)

- Forty-two percent of rape survivors told no one about the rape. (1)

- Forty-one percent of women who are raped expect to be raped again. (1)

- False reports of rape are rare, according to the FBI, occurring only 8 percent of the time. (13)

- Females aged 16–19 are four times more likely than the general population to be victims of rape, attempted rape, or sexual assault. (4)

- Rape survivors report defining their experience in many different ways. One-fourth define it as rape, one-fourth think it was a crime but did not know it was rape, one-fourth believe it was serious sexual abuse but did not know it was a crime, and one-fourth report not feeling victimized by the experience. (14)

Circumstances of Rape

- Fifty-seven percent of rapes happen on dates. (1)

- Seventy-five percent of the men and 55 percent of the women involved in acquaintance rapes were drinking or taking drugs just before the attack. (1)

- About 70 percent of sexual-assault survivors reported that they took some form of self-protective action during the crime. The most common technique was to resist by struggling or chase and try to hold the attacker. Of those survivors who took protective action, over half believed it helped the situation, about one-fifth believed that it made the situation worse or simultaneously worse and better. (7)

- Eighty-four percent of rape survivors tried unsuccessfully to reason with the man who raped her. (1)

- Fifty-five percent of gang rapes on college campuses are committed by fraternities, 40 percent by sports teams, and 5 percent by others. (15)

- Approximately 40 percent of sexual assaults take place in the survivor's home. About 20 percent occur in the home of a friend, neighbor, or relative. Ten percent occur outside, away from home. About 8 percent take place in parking garages. (7)

- More than half of all rape and sexual-assault incidents occurred within one mile of the survivor's home or in her home. (7)

What Happens After the Rape?

- In a study done in the 1980s, 5 percent of rape survivors went to the police. (1)

- Throughout the last 10 years, the National Crime Victimization Survey has reported that approximately 30 percent of rape survivors report the incident to the police. (4)

- Of those rapes reported to the police (which is 1/3 or less to begin with), only 16 percent result in prison sentences. Therefore, approximately 5 percent of the time, a man who rapes ends up in prison, 95 percent of the time he does not. (4)

- Forty-two percent of rape survivors had sex again with the rapist. (1)

- Thirty percent of rape survivors contemplate suicide after the rape. (1)

- Eighty-two percent of rape survivors say the rape permanently changed them. (1)

- The adult pregnancy rate associated with rape is estimated to be 4.7 percent. (17)

- Nongenital physical injuries occur in approximately 40 percent of rape cases. (18)

- Rape survivors often experience long-term symptoms of chronic headaches, fatigue, sleep disturbance, recurrent nausea. (19)

- Rape survivors often experience eating disorders and make suicide attempts after being raped. In addition, after being raped, survivors are 2½ times more likely than the average woman to have a substance-abuse problem. (20, 21, 22)

What Does *The Men's Program* Do About This?

■   *The Men's Program* has been shown to significantly decrease men's belief in rape myths by 50 percent after seeing the program. (23)

■   Seventy-five percent of high-risk men who see *The Men's Program* report being less likely to rape immediately after, and seven months after seeing *The Men's Program*. (24)

■   Men who see *The Men's Program* report a statistically significant decrease in their rape-myth acceptance and in their likelihood of raping immediately after and seven months after seeing the program. This decline lasts longer than that of any other program evaluated in the published research literature today. (24, 25)

Know how to answer the following:

■   The university has many resources available to sexual-assault survivors. Ten of these are listed on a course handout. Be able to name several of them.

■   Know how your university defines different types of sexual offenses and be able to distinguish among them.

■   Give one definition of a rape myth. Give an example or two of what a rape myth is. State several types of people who are more likely to believe rape myths (men, people with more traditional sex-role stereotypes, etc.). What do we know about differences between different racial groups concerning belief in rape myths?

■   A course handout describes 17 characteristics of sexual-assault offenders. What are several of these?

■   What are the four stages of rape-trauma syndrome. What are some of the basic and some of the specific characteristics of each stage?

■   What are some of the reasons why a college or university should implement *The Men's Program*? Of course there are lots of reasons to have a rape-prevention program, but what particular aspects of *The Men's Program* do research and theory suggest make the program worthwhile?

■   In your opinion, why does rape happen? Use course readings to support your answer.

■   Why is it difficult for women to report rape? Discuss this issue relying primarily on Chapter 8 of McEvoy's book. (14) In particular, discuss reasons given by victims for not reporting rapes to the police, what happens during an after-rape exam, ways to reduce the emotional burden on women during a police interview, and reasons why her complaint may be called "unfounded."

References

(1)   Warshaw, R. *I Never Called It Rape*. New York: HarperCollins Publishers, 1994.

(2)   Douglas, K. A. et al. "Results From the 1995 National College Health Risk Behavior Survey." *Journal of American College Health* 46 (1997): 55–66.

(3)   Tjaden, P., and N. Thoennes. "Prevalence, Incidence, and Consequences of Violence Against Women: Findings From the National Violence Against Women Survey," 2-5, Research in Brief, Washington, D.C.: National Institute of Justice, U.S. Department of Justice, 1998.

(4)   Rennison, C. M. "National Crime Victimization Survey, Criminal Victimization 2001: Changes 2000–2001 with Trends 1993–2001," Washington, D.C.: U.S. Department of Justice, Bureau of Justice Statistics, NCJ 187007, 2002.

(5)   Davis, T. C, G. Q. Peck, and J. M. Storment. "Acquaintance Rape and the High School Student." *Journal of Adolescent Health* 14 (1993): 220–24.

(6)   Koss, M. P., L. Hiese, and N. F. Russo. "The Global Health Burden of Rape." *Psychology of Women Quarterly* 18 (1994): 509–37.

(7)   Greenfeld, L. A. *Sex Offenses and Offenders: An Analysis of Data on Rape and Sexual Assault*, Washington D.C.: U.S. Department of Justice, Bureau of Justice Statistics, 1997.

(8)   Peterson, S. A., and B. Franzese. "Correlates of College Men's Sexual Abuse of Women." *Journal of College Student Personnel* 28 (1987): 223–28.

(9)   Malamuth, N. M. "Rape Proclivity Among Males." *Journal of Social Issues* 37 (1981): 138–57.

(10) National Center for Injury Prevention and Control. *Rape Fact Sheet*. Atlanta: Centers for Disease Control and Prevention, U.S. Department of Health and Human Services.

(11) Gray, N. B., G. J. Palileo, and G. D. Johnson. "Explaining Rape Victim Blame: A Test of Attribution Theory." *Sociological Spectrum* 13 (1993): 377–92.

(12) "Sexual Abuse of Boys," *Journal of the American Medical Association*, December 2, 1998.

(13) Federal Bureau of Investigation. *Uniform Crime Reports*. Washington, D.C.: United States Department of Justice, 1995.

(14) Koss, M. "Rape on Campus: Facts and Measures." *Planning for Higher Education* 20 (1992): 21–28.

(15) O'Sullivan, C. "Acquaintance Gang Rape on Campus." In A. Parrot and L. Bechhofer (eds.) *Acquaintance Rape: The Hidden Crime*. New York: John Wiley and Sons, 1991.

(16) Kilpatrick, D. G., C. N. Edmunds, and A. K. Seymour. *Rape in America: A Report to the Nation*. National Victim Center, 1992.

(17) Homes, M. M., H. S. Resnick, D. G. Kilpatrick, and C. L. Best. "Rape-related Pregnancy: Estimates and Descriptive Characteristics From a National Sample of Women." *American Journal of Obstetrics and Gynecology* 175 (1996): 320–24.

(18) Koss, M. P., and L. Heslet. "Somatic Consequences of Violence Against Women." *Archives of Family Medicine* 1 (1992): 53–59.

(19) Eby, K. K., J. C. Campbell, C. M. Sullivan, and W. S. Davidson. "Health Effects of Experiences of Sexual Violence for Women with Abusive Partners." *Health Care for Women International* 16/6 (1995): 563–76.

(20) Kilpatrick, D. G., C. L. Best, L. J. Veronen, A. E. Amick, L. A. Villeponteaux, and G. A. Ruff. "Mental Health Correlates of Criminal Victimization: A random Community Survey." *Journal of Consulting and Clinical Psychology* 53/6 (1985): 866–73.

(21) Resnick, H. S., R. Acierno, and D. G. Kilpatrick. "Health Impact of Interpersonal Violence to Medical and Mental Health Outcomes." *Behavioral Medicine* 23 (1997): 65–78.

(22) Kilpatrick, D. G., R. Acierno, H. S. Resnick, B. E. Saunders, and C. L. Best. "A Two-year Longitudinal Analysis of the Relationships Between Violent Assault and Substance Use in Women." *Journal of Consulting and Clinical Psychology* 65/5 (1997): 834–47.

(23) Foubert, J. D., and K. A. Marriott. "Effects of a Sexual Assault Peer Education Program on Men's Belief in Rape Myths." *Sex Roles* 36 (1997): 259–68.

(24) Foubert, J. D. "The Longitudinal Effects of a Rape-prevention Program on Fraternity Men's Attitudes, Behavioral Intent, and Behavior." *The Journal of American College Health* 48 (2000): 158–63.

(25) Schewe, P. A. "Guidelines for Developing Rape Prevention and Risk Reduction Interventions." In P. A. Schewe (ed.), *Preventing Violence in Relationships: Interventions Across the Life Span*. Washington, D.C.: American Psychological Association, 2002.

Handout #15

Interesting Responses We Get from Male Audiences*

Participant: "Yeah, but what about all those guys who are falsely accused?"

Facilitator: "Thanks for bringing this issue up. It's a big concern for many men. [According to the FBI, 92 percent of the time, women who report rape are telling the truth. Thus only 8 percent of rapes are false reports.]** If you're at all familiar with the reporting and trial procedures in rape cases, you're aware that a woman reporting may have to submit to a rape exam, a not so pleasant experience, as well as be subjected to all kinds of blaming questions. So a woman needs to be willing to put herself through quite a bit of hassle when reporting. If the reason for falsely accusing a man is to get back at him, or hurt him in some way, there are many methods to use that would be much less of a hassle. A woman once said that if she wanted to get back at some guy she could simply throw her wallet into a dumpster and say he stole it. … My advice to you: If you're with a woman and you fear that she may accuse you of sexually assaulting her, I suggest you carefully examine your behavior to see why you think she might do that. And examine exactly why you're with this person. If this is a big fear of yours, protect yourself. An effective way to do this is to establish *verbal consent* for each new level of intimacy you enter into with your date/partner."

Participant: "But what about when a woman gets a guy so excited that he can't stop."

Facilitator: "I hear what you're saying, and I agree that it can be *uncomfortable* to slow down or stop when sexually stimulated, *but* men can stop, no matter how worked up they are, whenever they decide to. Imagine a scenario: You're in high school, your girlfriend's parents are gone for the evening, you both decide to play some tonsil hockey on the living-room couch, things start getting hot, you reach the point where you're too excited to stop (wherever this may be), suddenly, the front door opens and in walk your girlfriend's parents. Now, do you think you would need to ejaculate first, or would you *decide* to stop right away?"

Participant: "What about those women who wear clothes that just advertise the fact that they want it. You can't tell me they're not partially responsible for rape then."

Facilitator: "Yes I can. If you're talking about men getting sexually stimulated when they see an attractive looking woman, I understand where you're coming from. I've certainly experienced that. But it's one thing to objectify a woman for your own pleasure (which is something we should talk about, too), and quite another to decide to act on those feelings without the consent of the other person. The perpetrator is *solely* responsible for sexually assaulting someone. Incidentally, as a man, I'm offended at the notion that men can't control themselves at the sight of an attractive woman."

---

*With permission of the publisher from *Men Stopping Rape*, Madison Wis.: Joe Weinberg of Weinberg and Associates.
**Bracketed text is updated information by John Foubert.

Participant: "Many say rape is about power and control and not sex, what do you think?

Facilitator: "When talking about this issue, it's important to separate the victim's experience from the perpetrator's. I think it's safe to say when a person is sexually assaulted, they feel overpowered and controlled. When men rape, they are definitely using power to control/dominate someone. However, these men may also feel as though they're just having sex. This makes more sense if we look back at how men learn and talk about sex. When men learn that sex is a conquest, a hunt, a game, and an achievement, it is difficult for them to separate it from power and control."

Participant: "Men and women just need to learn to communicate better."

Facilitator: "I agree that if men and women would use more verbal communication regarding sex, some things would be cleared up, but it goes beyond that. Many survivors clearly said 'no' and many tried to fight off the perpetrators. This is pretty clear communication to me."

Handout #16

Thoughts on Male Privilege for Men to Ponder

When we consider all of the privileges that our social system gives us, it can be quite startling to think of how we live our lives in the midst of privilege we don't always recognize. How often do we think about how we can be pretty sure of having our voice heard in a group in which we are the only member of our gender or how when we are told about our national heritage or about "civilization," that we are shown that people of our gender made it what it is. How often do we consider that we, as men, can think over many options, social, political, imaginative, or professional, without asking whether a person of our gender would be accepted or allowed to do what we want to do.

Yet to have some people be privileged and other people not privileged on the basis of something like gender, creates a system in which conflict, tension, and adversarial relationships are inherent. It is important for us as men to recognize that we have been granted privileges by our society that deserve to be shared equally with women, and in sharing them they cease to become privileges. Rather, they become shared resources.

To protect and to maintain these privileges within our own gender perpetuates a societal structure that allows women to be put in a submissive place and men to rule over them. When men are told they rule over women, they can come to believe that they are entitled to sex with whom they want and when they want. This attitude has dangerous and damaging consequences—20 times every hour in our country alone.

I believe that it is up to us, as men, to work toward egalitarian relationships between men and women. It is up to us to educate other men about their power and to encourage them to relinquish it in favor of equality. It is also up to us to relinquish this power in our own relationships with women.

I believe that as we do this we will find that our relationships with women will become more equal, less adversarial, more fully intimate, open, rewarding, and fulfilling. As Theodore Roosevelt said, "This country will not be a good place for any of us to live in unless we make it a good place for all of us to live in."

Let us all ponder these thoughts as we determine how best to go forth and make a difference.

Handout #17

Characteristics of Offenders

- Have had sexual experiences earlier than their nonoffending counterparts. (1)

- Believe more strongly in sex-role stereotyping. (2)

- Have more negative attitudes toward women. (1)

- Have higher rates of alcohol consumption. (2)

- Are more accepting of rape myths. (2)

- Perceive themselves as having been hurt more often by women, as having been deceived, betrayed, and manipulated. (3)

- Are more attuned to power dynamics between men and women. (3)

- More often feel put down, belittled, ridiculed, and mothered by women and more often feel the need to assert themselves because of this. (3)

- Are more impulsive and more apt to perceive themselves as losing control under the influence of alcohol. (3)

- Voice less respect for society's rules. (3)

- Discuss their sexual experiences with their peers more frequently than other men. (3)

- Will almost always report that their behavior that meets the legal definition of rape was "definitely not rape." (4)

(1) Koss, M. P., and T. E. Dinero. "Predictors of Sexual Aggression Among a National Sample of Male College Students." *Annals of the New York Academy of Science* 528 (1989): 133–46.

(2) Muehlenhard, C. L., and M. A. Linton. "Date Rape and Sexual Aggression in Dating Situations: Incidence and Risk Factors." *Journal of Counseling Psychology* 34/2 (1987): 186–96.

(3) Lisak, D., and S. Roth. Motivational Factors in Nonincarcerated Sexually Aggressive Men: Personality Processes and Individual Differences." *Journal of Personality and Social Psychology* 55/5 (1988): 795–802.

(4) Koss, M. P., C. A. Gidycz, and N. Wisniewski. "The Scope of Rape: Incidence and Prevalence of Sexual Aggression and Victimization in a National Sample of Higher Education Students." *Journal of Consulting and Clinical Psychology* 55 (1987): 162–70.

Handout #18

Lecture Notes for Article by Lonsway (1996)

Lonsway (1996)

Lonsway (1996) reviewed 20 years worth of research on rape-prevention programs. She found that coeducational rape-prevention programs tend to focus on cross-sex communication and dating expectations. Evaluation of such programs tends to focus on change that occurs right afterward and often only measures whether the audience enjoyed the presentation, rather than whether it changed their attitudes. Out of 15 coeducational programs, she found six that showed no change in men, four showed immediate change only, two limited their assessment to students' satisfaction with the program, two were based on semester-length classes showing little change, and one made men worse.

When Lonsway (1996) reviewed all-male programs, she found that most succeed but measured only the immediate programmatic effects. She believes that all-male programs offer greater promise for rape prevention. Out of seven all-male programs reviewed, one induced short-term change, three had immediate effects, two limited their assessment to students' satisfaction with the program, and one made men worse.

Lonsway found that effective rape-prevention programs tend to do the following:

- Allow time for interactive participation

- Discuss gender roles and the status of women

- Increase empathy for rape victims

- Use an approach that confronts ideology, not the person

- Use all-male environments

- Use peer educators

Handout #19

Discussion Questions for *Sexual Assault in Context** by Dr. Christopher Kilmartin

The following are some questions you can use to help students process the material in *Sexual Assault in Context*. After each question are my comments. I do not encourage you to read these comments to the students unless you think it might be helpful to do so in some instance, but the comments may help you to guide the discussion.

1. **Why is it important to talk about the history of gender and the forces that form gender?**

    We all live with the pressure to behave in ways that the culture considers "appropriate" for men or women. Men (and women) need to understand that 1) conforming to these pressures sometimes has negative consequences, 2) you can choose to resist these pressures if it is important for you to do so, and 3) regardless of what you choose, you are responsible for the consequences of your behavior.

    Psychologist Sandra Bem refers to gender as a set of "default options" that the culture attempts to program into us. Like the default options on your computer, changing your gender focus requires three conditions: 1) you have to know that they are default options and therefore it is possible to change them (if they are "hard wired," they only change with physical intervention—my belief is that most gendered behavior is learned), 2) you have to be motivated to change them, and 3) you have to know how to change them. Learning about gender is one way to fulfill the first condition—to give people a language for understanding gender pressure and thus an opportunity to take a critical look at this pressure and evaluate their options. It is very difficult to resist a pressure that you cannot name and it is also difficult to resist a pressure when you do not know where it comes from.

    I often tell audiences that sending college students out into the world without gender awareness is like sending them out without computer skills. Because of the forces that impel gender arrangement described in the book and the dynamic process of change in these forces, gender awareness, like computer skills, will only increase in importance as time goes on. College students who undertake a study of gender will improve their potential for functioning well in work, relationships, mental and physical health, and critical thinking skills. They also improve their potential for contributing to sexual-assault prevention, which is as much a lifestyle as it is a discrete set of behaviors.

---

*Note: Book and discussion questions written by Christopher Kilmartin, professor of Psychology, Mary Washington College, Fredericksburg, VA 22401, (540) 654–1562, ckilmart@mwc.edu.

2. What kinds of stories from your own life come up as you think about gender arrangements?

Storytelling is one way that we make sense of our lives. One person's story may change or stimulate others. Because gender pressure is universal, everyone has stories of their own, and telling them to each other helps us to make sense of our experiences and feelings.

3. What kinds of feelings come up as you think about gender arrangements?

Gender is an emotionally charged topic, and people who engage in discussions about it respond with a variety of feelings: some are angry, some are sad, others feel sentimental, happy, or anxious, and some have general feelings of emotional arousal that they cannot identify as belonging to a specific feeling.

Some men who engage in these discussions respond by becoming angry. They sometimes say it is "male bashing" and disrespectful to them. As one man put it, "I felt like you were telling me that I should be a certain way, and what if I don't want to be that way?" I don't want to take your choices away from you, but I do want your choices to be conscious ones rather than merely "going along with the program." Hypermasculine conformity can have dire consequences for college men: it can have negative effects on their physical safety, grades, alcohol use, friendships, and the way that they treat women.

4. How does gender information relate to your own life?

Sometimes people report that learning about gender influences them to see themselves in different ways and/or to resolve to behave differently. Others see little connection with their own lives. An additional question might be "How does learning about gender relate to your life as a college student?" This may be an opportunity to point out that several chronic problems on college campuses are related to "hypermasculine ideologies" (beliefs that men should be tough, unemotional, dominant, and aggressive), including substance abuse, physical risk-taking, and sexual assault.

5. What were the gendered arrangements in your parents' generation? How are yours going to be the same? Different?

This leads into a discussion about how the world is changing with regard to gender. Because of the changing character of the world of labor and because of reproductive technologies, there is virtually no work that men can do and women can't, and vice versa. This means that heterosexual couples will increasingly share all work both inside and outside of the home, and that gender will continue to decrease as an organizing principle of working and domestic life (which students have seen as a trend, even in their short lives). Holding on to antiquated notions of gendered arrangements will become more and more difficult.

6. What does all this have to do with sexual assault?

Sexual assault is associated with negative hypermasculine ("macho") ideologies, especially the toxic beliefs that women are inferior to men, like to be dominated, say "no" when they mean "yes", are available for men's sexual pleasure, and deserve to be assaulted when they get drunk, dress provocatively, or flirt. Men at risk for committing sexual assault tend to believe that their sexuality and aggressive urges are out of control, and they blame the victim for the assault. These men tend to associate with like-minded men, and hypermasculine peers support these ideologies with their use of sexist humor, pornography, denigration of women, and granting of high group status for men who have impersonal sex with a lot of female partners. While most men will never commit a sexual assault, all men are peers who can either support or challenge these toxic beliefs. Therefore, men's role in preventing sexual assault goes well beyond merely refraining from the behavior, and a critical examination of antiquated modes of masculinity is a key component of violence prevention. Many men have never questioned or even discussed cultural masculinity, and so they carry it as a non-conscious ideology. Gender education is an attempt to make masculinity conscious as a first step in helping men to explore this vague essence that so strongly influences their behavior and their effects on others.

Handout #20

Rape Myths
by Bradford C. Perry, M.A.

Rape myth—attitudes and beliefs that are generally false but are widely and persistently held, and that serve to deny and justify sexual violence, particularly men's sexual violence against women

Rape myths can be divided into three basic types: myths about the assault itself, myths pertaining to the victim, and myths that relate to the offender. Below is an overview of some common rape myths, followed by "debunking" statements.

The Assault

MYTH: Rape results from an uncontrollable sexual urge of biological origin. Men rape impulsively out of biological need/evolutionary programming. ("He just couldn't help himself. . . ")

FACT: Rape is a crime of power, where sex is used as the weapon. It is, by definition, an act of violence. Rape is an expression of a desire to *control* someone else's sexual decisions. This desire may be explicit ("Women are there for men's pleasure, thus they should do what I want.") or implicit ("It's too late for her to tell me 'no' now, I'm already too excited . . . "). This desire cannot be blamed on, or excused by, some sort of biological need or evolutionary trait.

- Almost 50 percent of convicted rapists were married or had potential sexual partners at the time of their offense(s) (Kilmartin 2000).

- Research has shown that the majority of rapes are planned, not impulsive (Lisak & Miller, in press; Thompson 2000).

- Some rapists need some form of sexual stimulation just before they penetrate their victim (if they are biologically programmed to rape, why isn't their biology "working").

- Most men do not commit rape, nor do they have the desire to commit rape.

MYTH: Rapes are usually reported.

FACT: Rape is the most underreported crime in the United States, with the FBI estimating that only 16 percent of rapes actually get reported (National Victim Center and Crime Victims Research and Treatment Center 1992).

MYTH: Husbands cannot rape their wives.

FACT: Rape occurs whenever a sexual act is performed without the freely given (i.e., not induced by threat, intoxication, etc.) consent of both partners. No relationship between the individuals can excuse such behavior, or override any lack of consent.

MYTH: Because of a few violent incidents, the issue of rape tends to be overblown—it's not really that big of a problem.

FACT: The estimated lifetime prevalence of rape and attempted rape is between 21 percent and 27 percent for women in industrialized nations (Koss, Heise, and Russo 1994). The 2000 U.S. National Crime Victimization Survey estimated that 246,000 women were the victims of rape in the year 2000. That is roughly equal to a rape every two minutes.

MYTH: Most rapes occur outside. They are perpetrated by someone who the victim does not know who jumps out of the bushes wielding a weapon, and commits the rape with a large degree of physical force and overt violence.

FACT: Over 50 percent of rapes occur in a residence, and in over 80 percent of rapes the victim knows the attacker (Warshaw 1994). Also, most rapists do not use any weapon except their greater physical size and weight to intimidate and/or overpower their victims. Alcohol is also frequently used to lessen the victim's ability to resist. Most rapists only use as much force as is necessary to hold their victim still and achieve penetration (Thompson 2000).

MYTH: Men cannot be raped.

FACT: Men, both heterosexual and gay, can be and are raped—usually by heterosexual men. Although the research findings on this are still unclear, it is estimated that between 5 percent and 10 percent of men will be the victims of sexual assault in their lifetimes (Scarce 1997). Of rape victims, the U.S. Department of Justice found that over 9 percent are male (U.S. Department of Justice, 1998).

The Victim

MYTH: When a woman says no, she is just playing "hard to get" and she really means yes.

FACT: If you are like me, you do not have the ability to read another person's mind. If a person says no, then that is all one can know about what sexual acts are OK with her or him—it should not be assumed that they "really mean yes." If it is unclear as to whether or not consent exists (i.e., if neither "yes" or "no" have been said), then it is the responsibility of the person initiating the sexual act to *ask*. Many rapists have used the defense, "C'mon, I knew she really wanted it, she was just putting on a show so that I didn't think she was a slut." One can only be sure what another person wants if they ask—a practice conspicuously absent from rapists. Regardless of what one person *thinks* another person wants, one cannot be sure until their partner communicates their desires clearly. Everyone has the right to control what happens to their own bodies.

MYTH: Sexual assault only happens to careless people who are "asking for it" by the way they dress, or by where they are.

FACT: Rape is a crime that often causes an indescribable amount of pain and suffering for the victim. Over 82 percent of randomly sampled rape survivors in the U.S. said that the rape permanently changed their lives, and over 30 percent of rape victims contemplate suicide in the aftermath of the rape (Warshaw 1994). No one asks for this to happen to them. All kinds of people—young, old, rich, poor, black, white, straight, gay, male, and female— are sexually assaulted in all kinds of places. The idea that victims provoke assault by their behavior assumes that they have no right to be as free as you or I. Even if you think a victim made poor decisions, bad judgment is not a rapeable offense. The "asking for it" myth shifts the blame from the perpetrator to the victim of this crime. The underlying motivation for engaging in this myth is often so that one can feel more secure—if the rapes happen because of something the victims are doing, then one can convince themselves that they can keep rape from happening to them by acting or not acting a certain way. This myth makes rape seem more controllable. In actuality however, the decision to rape is completely in the hands of the rapist. Only the rapist can control whether or not a rape is initiated against a potential victim, and thus responsibility for the rape falls firmly on the rapist's shoulders. This is why sexual assault is never a victim's fault—and no one deserves to be raped.

MYTH: If a person agrees to some degree of sexual intimacy, then he or she is willing to "go all the way."

FACT: Any person has the right to agree to any degree of sexual intimacy they feel comfortable with at that moment, and to not go any further if they do not wish to. A person may feel comfortable with one kind of sexual activity but not with another—or he or she may decide at any time that he or she is not really ready for further intimacy.

MYTH: "Nice" girls don't get raped. "Bad" girls shouldn't complain.

FACT: This is similar to the just-discussed "the victim must have been asking for it" myth, except that it focuses more on the extent of a victim's sexual experience. Like the "asking for it" myth, it serves to make people more secure by making rape seem more controllable. It also serves to punish promiscuous women by saying, "If you like to have a lot of sex, then you can't always pick and choose who your partners are." This is a particularly damning sentiment, and it plays into a double standard that is rampant in our culture. If a woman enjoys sex, and is open about her enjoyment, then she is often labeled as "easy." However, it is considered somewhat normal for men to be open about enjoying sex. Furthermore, men who have had many sexual partners are never called "sluts," but rather "ladies men" or "players." This double standard is damaging because it denies women any sexual assertiveness or autonomy. If women were allowed to openly express their sexuality (in whatever amount they individually see fit) then so many of the other rape myths would become moot. Defense attorneys could no longer argue, "She may have said 'no,' but that was just because she didn't want to appear easy." The media would have no interest in focusing on details like "The alleged perpetrator and the victim were seen flirting in a bar just hours before the rape . . ." These distractions would no longer carry any weight because there would no longer be a perception that women should always try to hide any sexual feelings that they might have.

MYTH: Women who don't fight back or scream must secretly want to be raped.

FACT: Most men are larger and stronger than most women. Also, many women are raised to avoid/calm tense or violent situations. These two factors, combined with the fact that a rapist will frequently ignore, and possibly forcefully retaliate against any hint of initial protest by the victim, provides great insight into why some victims do not put up an outward struggle (Thomson 2000). It is important to note that some victims may use more inward strategies to resist the rape psychologically. For instance, many victims will say that they just closed their eyes and prayed for it to be over—they make their mind go somewhere else so that they did not have to experience the rape.

MYTH: People often lie about being raped.

FACT: According to the FBI, the rate of false reporting in rape cases is no higher than 5–8 percent (see most recent *Uniform Crime Report*).

MYTH: People do not often report rape because they know they provoked it.

FACT: It takes a tremendous amount of courage to come forward and report a rape. Besides risking a social stigma of "damaged goods," victims also tend to worry about how their friends, family, and romantic partner will react. Many victims do not come forward for fear that a father, brother, or boyfriend will go out and try to get revenge, possibly ending-up injured or incarcerated. Teenage and college-aged victims may worry that their parents will blame them for drinking (if alcohol was involved) and/or become overprotective and restrictive of their freedom. Victims of acquaintance rape may also face harsh reprisals from their social group, who will either side strongly with the victim or strongly with the perpetrator (who is often from the same social group). Given all of these obstacles, it is no wonder rape is such an underreported crime.

MYTH: No person could survive a rape without at least losing their sanity.

FACT: While it is true that rape will likely permanently alter the life of a survivor, this does not mean that the rape will cause some sort of living death sentence. The psychological trauma of rape can be healed in time, and the survivor can go on to lead a happy and satisfying life. A rape survivor needs support, understanding, and the opportunity to deal with the aftermath of the rape, sometimes with the help of a counselor, or with the help of other people who have gone through a similar experience.

MYTH: A prostitute will not be traumatized by rape. After all, having sex is her job.

FACT: A sexual assault can be just as traumatic to an experienced prostitute as to anyone else, and he or she has as much right to treatment, protection, and justice. Remember, rape is a crime of violence and power, not simply a sexual act gone awry. It can be just as painful for a prostitute to experience a loss of control over her body and her sexual decisions as a virgin.

MYTH: Sexual assault is impossible without some cooperation from the victim (AKA "it's hard to thread a moving needle" theory).

FACT: Many rapists are willing to use all of the force necessary to accomplish penetration, even when it is physically injurious to the victim. Even a struggling victim can be penetrated if they are pinned against the ground or a wall. In cases where the victim does not resist out of fear or for some other reason, her submission is not the same as cooperation. If she chooses to cooperate because of the rapist's threats to her or others, her cooperation is not the same as consent.

MYTH: In a rape, the person who is raped is the only one who suffers.

FACT: Sexual assault affects the victim's family, friends, and neighbors. The fear of sexual assault affects all women. Watching the survivor go through the aftermath of a rape commonly causes immense pain in everyone close to the survivor, particularly romantic partners. It is also the most costly crime to our society—according to the U.S. Department of Justice, the crime of sexual assault costs America **127 billion dollars** every year (combined medical/mental health care, police/EMS response, and social/victim services costs; excludes costs of investigation, prosecution, and incarceration).

The Offender

MYTH: A large percentage of rapes are interracial (black men raping white women).

FACT: FBI statistics have shown that less than 10 percent of reported rapes are interracial, although the exact percentage varies according to the area. This myth has become less prevalent with the rise of more egalitarian relationships between whites and blacks (see most recent *Uniform Crime Reports*).

MYTH: Most rapists are "insane."

FACT: Although some rapists have been shown to have hypermasculine tendencies, and/or a propensity towards violence, most are **not** suffering from any diagnosable psychological disorder. Most rapists seem very normal in their day-to-day behavior.

MYTH: Men who rape other men are gay.

FACT: The vast majority of males who assault other males are heterosexual (Groth and Burgess 1980). Men and women are assaulted for basically the same reasons: so that the assailant can vent hostility/feel a sense of power/control the situation to his desired outcome. It is important to note that a fear or disdain for homosexuality ironically motivates some men to rape gay men.

References

Groth, N. A., and A. W. Burgess. "Male Rape: Offenders and Victims." *American Journal of Psychiatry* 137 (1980).

Kilmartin, C. Personal communication, 2000.

Koss, M. P., L. Heise, and N. F. Russo. "The Global Health Burden of rape." *Psychology of Women Quarterly* 18 (1994): 509–37.

Lisak, D., and P. M. Miller. "Repeat Rape and Multiple Offending Among Undetected Rapists," (in press). *Violence and Victims.*

National Victim Center and Crime Victims Research and Treatment Center. "Rape in America: A Report to the Nation," 1992.

Scarce, M. *Male on Male Rape: The Hidden Toll of Stigma and Shame.* New York: Insight, 1997.

Thompson, S. "Behavioral Profile of Acquaintance Rapists." Paper presented at the Tenth International conference on Sexual Assault and Harassment on Campus. Orlando, Fla., October 2000.

U.S. Department of Justice (1996). "Victim Costs and Consequences: A New Look."

U.S. Department of Justice (1998). "Bureau of Justice Statistics Report on Crime Victimization in 1998."

Warshaw, R. *I Never Called It Rape.* New York: Harper Collins, 1994.

Handout #21

Results of a Seven-month Study of *The Men's Program*

- Rape-myth acceptance declined significantly, immediately after the program.

- Rape-myth acceptance remained significantly lower seven months after the program.

- Rape-myth acceptance was significantly lower in the program group than the control group seven months later, with no rebound.

- Likelihood of raping declined significantly immediately after the program.

- Likelihood of raping remained significantly lower seven months after the program with no rebound.

- Twenty percent of participants reported some likelihood of raping prior to the program.

- Of that 20 percent, 75 percent reported less likelihood of raping after the program, the remaining 25 percent stayed the same.

- According to an independent review of the research literature, *The Men's Program* is the only program to report clear, long-term positive effects (Schewe 2002).

Handout #22

Why Using a Male-on-Male Rape Scenario is Appropriate in Educating Men About Sexual Assault

⊠ **How do the police rape-training video produced by NO MORE and *The Men's Program* describe a male-on-male rape scenario?**

The NO MORE video refers to one attacker as being married and the other as having a girlfriend—establishing their sexual orientation as presumably heterosexual. This allows us to emphasize the violence of the attack and puts the emphasis on what many male-on-male rape situations involve: a heterosexual perpetrator.

The script for "The Men's Program" reinforces the presumed heterosexuality of the rapists, and uses this to reinforce male-on-male rape as an act of violence where many perpetrators are presumably heterosexual.

⊠ **How are other stimulus tools used?**

Many programs show or describe a male-on-female rape situation. Does this practice promote violence against women and/or misogyny? Of course not. Would we show a male-on-female rape scenario without framing, disclaiming, and processing? No. Why not? It doesn't warn people, there is no context set for why we show it, it could reinforce people's perceptions. Also, what if we showed another kind of video that described something painful and/or hurtful—for example a speech that was antiSemitic. Are there contexts within an institution where this could be useful as a teaching tool? Yes, to teach people about the effects of hate and what it can lead to as referenced by the holocaust. Would we just show an antiSemitic video without framing, disclaiming, and processing? Of course not.

⊠ **What is homophobia?**

Homophobia is described in many ways. Most often the definition involves an irrational fear of activity and/or people who are gay, lesbian, bisexual, or transgendered.

⊠ **Why and how should we process a male-on-male scenario?**

Stimulus tools are all in how we as educators use them to teach others. We know (through nine studies) that the only technique so far that has been shown to affect men's long-term likelihood of raping is to discuss a male-on-male rape scenario. Some men in our audience are probably homophobic. Do we then not discuss this scenario because some might be homophobic? No. Talking about male-on-male rape is not something that is homophobic by nature. Discussing this scenario appropriately can both reduce the likelihood of raping and it also gives us the chance to educate men in a way that confronts a common homophobic misperception—that male-on-male rape is motivated by sexual desire and is most commonly done by a homosexual man. This belief is not true, and we confront this misperception with *The Men's Program*. If we did not make the sexual orientation of the men in the video clear, this could be problematic; but we do. We also make sure that it is described (in the video and in processing) as a violent act by nature committed by presumably heterosexual men. Thus, we use the male-on-male rape scenario as a teaching tool to help men understand rape more fully, empathize with survivors, and identify rape as an act of violence.

⊠ **What is one possible way to answer the question "Is there any concern that describing a male-on-male scenario might bring up any issues of homophobia?"**

No, not with the way we do our program. We have to remember that rape is primarily an act of violence. What is depicted on the video is clearly a violent act. One of the things we do in our program is combat any pre-existing homophobic attitudes among members of the audience. A common manner in which homophobia manifests itself is that if a man is raped, his attacker must be a homosexual man. The video we use describes a situation in which a man is raped by presumably heterosexual men, thus helping debunk the myth men who rape men are necessarily homosexual. In addition, we hit this point home immediately after the video concludes by noting that the perpetrators were presumably heterosexual, as with many male-on-male rape situations. Thus, we work to attenuate homophobia, not perpetuate it. Also, think about this for a second. Many programs for women have focused on describing women being raped and the effects it has on them, but these programs surely don't perpetuate misogyny and violence against women just because they talk about women who are raped. In the same way, our program does not perpetuate homophobia or any other type of violence. In fact, in one of the studies on the program it was found that our program has no effect on homophobia at all. Also, when asked to write about how the program impacted their attitudes and/or behavior, no respondent in a comprehensive evaluation study of the program wrote any comment that would even remotely suggest that the program was interpreted as homophobic. Thus, whether we pursue this question from a philosophical, logical, or research basis, the answer is the same.

Handout #23

How to Handle Difficult People and Questions

Advice About Techniques in General

- Ask that questions wait until the end of the program. Call first on people who raised their hands in the middle, if applicable.

- Unless the person is so out of control that dialogue is clearly not possible, make sure you understand the question and convince the person that you hear their concern.

- Use a combination of logic, your experience, your knowledge of facts, and affirming his right to his opinion of the matter.

- Use your fellow presenters, step in and support each other.

- Find a place of agreement and move on when necessary.

- Offer to talk with the person further after the program is over.

- Offer to get the person more information or discuss the matter more thoroughly at a later time.

- Use others in the audience to confront the difficult person.

- See Handout #15 for sample questions and responses.

If a woman comes to an all-male performance, be sensitive to her desire to attend while finding a way to maintain the all-male nature of the program. Find a way to talk with her privately, let her know that this presentation is being done for an all-male audience. Be sure to make these three points:

- Research shows the program works best in an all-male environment.

- Offer her the chance to see the program at a time when you are not performing for a particular all-male audience.

- Ask if she has any questions and make sure you give her a resource flyer to insure that she has resources available to her.

Handout #24

Suggested Answers for a Variety of Questions

⊠ Why don't you let women present with you or see the program?

Everything about our program is based on what has been shown by the research literature to be most effective. The research is conclusive that when you talk to college men about rape, the most effective way is in all-male audiences with male peer educators presenting. One of the things you often find in coeducational programs is that men try to impress the women in the room, try to antagonize them, or shut down and don't listen for fear of having their opinions attacked. None of these reactions help men learn about this important issue. *The Men's Program* focuses on empowering men to learn how to help women recover from rape—*treating them as potential helpers not as potential rapists.* We do this in an environment where they can safely ask questions and not feel defensive with women in the room. Any time a woman wants to see our program we make sure she has an opportunity to do so. When we present to men though, we try to do this in an all-male environment given its proven efficacy as demonstrated by several research studies.

⊠ How do you know this program works?

We've seen it work in our experience and we've read the research proving that it lowers men's rape-myth acceptance and likelihood of raping for at least an academic year. Before *The Men's Program*, the most effective rape-prevention programs that were evaluated changed men's attitudes for up to two months and their likelihood of raping for only one day. No program was reported to go beyond these levels. Research on *The Men's Program* found that it led to a statistically significant change in both attitudes and likelihood of raping for seven months. What is even more startling is that among "high-risk" men (those most likely to rape), 75 percent of them report being less likely to rape after seeing the program. So, we are able to reach those men best who we need to reach the most. These results are published in the book *The Men's Program* and are reported in an article in the *Journal of American College Health*. Additional research on *The Men's Program* found that men also significantly improve their ability to help women recover from rape. Thus, *The Men's Program* has a dual benefit—we make men better able to help women recover from rape, and at the same time make men less likely to be perpetrators in the first place.

⊠ Do you ever get any criticism of the program?

The most common reaction we get from people is overwhelming support. We are a bunch of male student leaders who are working proactively to end rape with a program that's proven to work. Every once in a while people will question its all-male format. Once we explain that we do our program the way we do because research shows it works best—and that women can see the program if they want to—the over-whelming majority of people who question this aspect end up strongly supporting us. On the whole, the program has very strong support and is spreading quickly across the country.

⊠ **Your video is very powerful. How do guys react to it?**

Stunned silence. They really learn what it might feel like to be raped. Through it, we build the empathy men need to really understand what it is like to be overpowered, controlled, and violated. Research shows that rape-prevention programs that use an empathy-based intervention work far better than those that just present guys with facts or statistics. Also, when you look at the research on different rape-prevention pro-grams, it is clear that empathy-based programs describing a man as a survivor are the most effective way to improve men's attitudes and lower their likelihood of raping. They learn that rape is a crime of violence, that it hurts, that it's violating. They see in a new way what it's like to be overpowered—to be raped. It's important to keep in mind that empathy is a distinct feeling state. It requires participating in the experience of the other, through having a similar experience directly or through imagination. It is the sharing of the experience that permits a sharing of the feelings and needs which emerge in response to the experience. Once we get men to understand what a rape feels like through this video, they are much better able to understand what women often go through and how best to help these women, if women come to them asking for help.

⊠ **Is there any concern that describing a male-on-male scenario might bring up any issues of homophobia?**

No, not with the way we do our program. We have to remember that rape is primarily an act of violence. What is depicted on the video is clearly a violent act. One of the things we do in our program is combat any pre-existing homophobic attitudes among members of the audience. A common manner in which homophobia manifests itself is that if a man is raped, his attacker must be a homosexual man. The video we use describes a situation in which a man is raped by presumably heterosexual men, thus helping debunk the myth men who rape men are homosexual. In addition, we hit this point home immediately after the video concludes by noting that the perpetrators were presumably heterosexual, as with many male-on-male rape situations. Thus, we work to attenuate homophobia, not perpetuate it. Also, think about this for a second. Many programs for women have focused on describing women being raped and the effects it has on them, but these programs surely don't perpetuate misogyny and violence against women just because they talk about women who are raped. In the same way, our program does not perpetuate homophobia or any other type of violence. In fact, in one of the studies on the program it was found that our program has no effect on homophobia at all. Also, when asked to write about how the program impacted their attitudes and/or behavior, no respondent in a comprehensive evaluation study of the program wrote any comment that would even remotely suggest that the program was interpreted as homophobic. Thus, whether we pursue this question from a philosophical, logical, or research basis, the answer is the same.

Other potential questions you might be asked:

⊠ How did you hear about this group?

⊠ Why did you decide to join this group?

⊠ What do you hope the group will accomplish?

⊠ What do you personally hope to gain from being a member?

⊠ How do your fellow students react to you being a member of "One in Four" (how do guys react, how do women react)?

⊠ How often do you guys present?

⊠ Was there some experience that led to your interest in this cause?

Handout #25

Survivor Empathy

The use of empathy in rape awareness and prevention programs is one of the most discussed issues in rape prevention today. Empathy is a distinct feeling state. It requires participating in the experience of the other, through having a similar experience directly or through imagination. It is the sharing of the experience which permits a sharing of the feelings and needs that emerge in response to that experience. Barring an actual rape experience, true empathy is difficult if not impossible without discussing a rape situation that an audience can relate to in a very real and personal way.

Nine studies have been published that assessed the effects of an empathy-based intervention on men' attitudes toward rape and/or their behavioral intent to rape. Six of these studies (Foubert 2000; Foubert and Marriott 1997; Foubert and McEwen 1998; Gilbert, Heesacker, and Gannon 1991; Lee 1987; and Schewe and O'Donohue 1993) have assessed the impact of depicting a man as a survivor. Three studies (Berg 1993; Berg, Lonsway, and Fitzgerald 1999; Ellis, O'Sullivan, and Sowards 1992) depicted a woman as a survivor. All six studies depicting a man as a survivor significantly improved men's attitudes toward rape and/or their behavioral intent to rape. In stark contrast, *all* of the studies evaluating the impact of describing a woman's experience as a survivor *increased* men's rape-myth acceptance, and in the case of Berg (1993), also *increased* men's likelihood of sexual aggression.

Handout #26

The Male Box*

Objectives

- To illustrate how society constructs gender roles for boys and men that may have a negative impact on their behavior and development (e.g. men's violence against women, other men, and themselves.

- To encourage boys and men to define their own individual identities.

- To encourage boys and men to stand up for others who may not fit into socially constructed gender roles.

Time: 25 minutes

Introduction

Ask the participants the difference between gender and sex (you are born with your sex, assigned your gender). Then, ask the participants how we learn to be men (media, parents, teachers, coaches, peers—all parts of what we define collectively as *society*).

Exercise

Draw a large box on the board and write "To Be a Man" at the top. Ask the participants, "What does society stereotypically say it means to be a man?" Responses should fall into the following categories and include:

- Relationships with women (dominant, player, in charge)

- Attitude (tough, unemotional, hard)

- Possessions (car, money, job, women)

- Sexuality (heterosexual, "player," not gay)

- Behaviors (drinking, playing sports, having sex, fighting)

Then ask, "What names would a boy or man be called if he steps outside of the box? (responses will generally include: fag, pussy, weak, woman, bitch). Facilitate a discussion using the following:

- What do all the words outside of the box have in common (all negative associations with women and gay men)?

- Why are these words used (to insult, imply weakness)?

- What message does this send to men (girls and women are inferior to men)?

- How does this impact men's attitude and behavior towards women?

- How does a group that believes another group is inferior typically treat that group (poorly, with no respect)?

Make specific connections between words inside of the box and words outside of the box such as, "If a man cries, he is called a pussy." By using this word, men are discouraged from expressing their emotions. The use of this word also equates weakness with women.

Finally, ask "What harmful things do men and boys do to stay in or get back into the box" (e.g., verbal and physical challenges, suppression of emotions, risk-taking behavior, pressure and stress to attain lofty goals, oppression of underprivileged groups)?

Conclusion

Emphasize the following points to participants:

- Define your own identity.

- It is OK to have some of the qualities/characteristics that are inside the box as long as it is your decision, not a response to conform to a socially prescribed gender norm.

- As leaders, support other boys and men who may choose to be outside of the box.

Appendix D
Sample Recruitment Materials

Sample Letter to Colleagues Inviting
Nominations for "One in Four" Members

Date

Dear Colleague,

I am writing to ask for your assistance in identifying potential candidates for an all-male, sexual-assault, peer-education group that is being created here at (your university).

A new peer-education group is being created to present a program called "How to Help a Sexual-Assault Survivor: What Men Can Do." The new group will present this program to men in residence halls, fraternities, athletic teams, and any other group who will listen.

The one-hour workshop these men will learn to present is designed to help undergraduate men learn how to help a woman recover from a rape experience. The tone of the program is empowering, not blaming in nature. As this new group teaches men how to help their women friends recover from rape, audience members also become significantly less likely to rape in the first place. A recently published study found that 75 percent of high-risk men who see this program report a lower likelihood of raping—an effect that lasts, significantly, for seven months. In short, its the most effective rape-prevention program evaluated in the research literature today. An added benefit is that men who see it learn how to help a friend recover from a rape experience. This new group will be selected, trained, and advised by (name or names of people).

Ideal candidates are sophomore and junior men who are 1) strong public speakers, 2) relate well to other men, and 3) are sensitive to issues of violence against women. Exceptional freshmen men and seniors who will be here for another year or who want to continue their work after graduation will be considered. On the back of this letter, in an e-mail, or on a sheet of paper, would you please write down the names of students you think would be good for this group? If you have their address and phone number, that would be great too, but I can look them up if needed.

Please send your nominations to (name, address, e-mail, phone). Please send these names by October 23 or sooner, if possible.

Please call anytime with any questions. Thank you in advance for your assistance.

Sincerely,

Your name

Sample Letter to Send to Men Nominated for Membership in "One in Four"

Date

Dear,

I am writing you with news of an opportunity for you to make a tangible difference in the lives of many people, most of all, your own. As part of my role as (your title here), I am creating a new all-male, sexual-assault, peer-education group here on campus. I'm writing you because you have been nominated by (name of nominator) to be interviewed to be a founding member of this new group. I hope you will take the time to read further about what this opportunity may mean for you.

Back in 1993, a program was designed with one basic goal: to empower men to take a positive role in ending the suffering caused by rape. Too many programs dealing with rape treated men as potential rapists. The program we will use treats men as potential helpers. "How to Help a Sexual-Assault Survivor: What Men Can Do," is a training workshop for college men designed to teach them how awful rape feels, how they can help their women friends recover from rape, and how they as men can take more responsibility for ending rape. The program itself is most effective when undergraduate men present it to undergraduate men. That's where you may fit into this picture.

I would like to interview you, and many other nominees, as a part of a selective process to choose the best men on campus to be founding members of a new peer-education group. This group will present the program I mentioned all over campus, and perhaps beyond.

There are a few details that may interest you. This program has recently been shown to do many things. First, it significantly improves men's ability to help women recover from rape. Secondly, recently published research proves that it is the most effective rape prevention program ever evaluated in published research literature. In short, 75 percent of high-risk men who see the program report that they become less likely to rape—an effect that lasts for at least an academic year. No other program has ever been shown to be even nearly this effective.

Few things in life are guaranteed but I think I can guarantee you a few things. One is that if you are selected to be in this group, your life will be different from before. I can also guarantee you beyond any reasonable doubt that if you present this program, every time you do so, you will change the lives of the men who see it, and indirectly, the lives of many women too. I hope to be able to tell you more about this.

If you are interested in an interview please call me for more information. Interviews will take place between October 26 and November 5.

Sincerely,

Your name

Attachment to Enclose With Letter to Send Men Who Agree to Interview

Please come to your interview prepared to talk about yourself and your opinions, and to present the following information. The information you see in bold print will be provided for you on a large presenter's poster.

To start off, we'll go over a couple definitions.

The first definition we'd like to go over is for *sexual assault*. The definition we use for sexual assault is a broad one, and includes many different types of behavior. As you can see:

Sexual assault—Sexual intercourse without consent, forcible sodomy, sexual penetration with an object, intentionally touching an unwilling person's intimate parts, or forcing an unwilling person to touch another's intimate parts. These acts occur by force, threat, surprise, intimidation, or by taking advantage of someone's helplessness or inability to consent.

So basically what this definition of sexual assault includes would be having intercourse with someone who doesn't agree to it or can't agree to it. It also includes oral sex, anal sex, penetrating someone with an object, touching someone's intimate parts or making them touch your intimate parts when they don't agree to do so and/or are forced to do so.

Rape is a more specific kind of sexual assault. The U.S. Department of Justice, defines rape as:

Rape—sexual intercourse by force or against that person's will, or where the victim is incapable of giving consent given the persons age or temporary or permanent mental or physical incapacity.

So you can see that rape would be having intercourse with someone when they don't agree to it or are forced into it, or are unable to agree to it. Cases of rape also fit the broader definition of sexual assault, but not all sexual-assault cases meet the definition of rape.

Particularly in the case of rape, some people think that the most common type of rape happens when a guy a woman doesn't know grabs her by surprise and rapes her somewhere. While rape by a stranger does occur sometimes, we want you to remember this:

Four out of five times when a woman is raped, it is by someone she knows. It could be an acquaintance. It could be a friend. It could be a date. But four out of five times, it is someone she knows. And the average length of time she has known him is one year. Not just a few weeks, but on average, it's been one year.

Sample of Letter to Send Men Who Agree to Interview

Dear (name of interviewee),

I enjoyed talking with you and am glad that you are interested in interviewing to be a founding member of (name of your institution's first all-male, sexual-assault, peer-education group to present *The Men's Program*. The experience promises to be fun, challenging, meaningful, and a lot of hard work. If you're up to it, please read on.

During your interview, you will be asked to talk about your interest in being a peer educator. You will also be asked to give a very brief presentation using the attached hand-out as a guide. It's OK to read from this script during your interview. I want to gauge your presentation style, not your knowledge level or ability to memorize.

I hope to conclude the selection process on (insert appropriate date here), and I hope to notify people around (insert appropriate date here) about their status. If you become part of this group, I assure you that you will make a difference in the lives of others. I can think of few other experiences that offer you the same opportunity. I will pledge myself to the group to challenge and support each member throughout their experience—an experience that will make a profound impact upon all those involved.

I look forward to our interview time. See you then.

Sincerely,

Your name here

Suggested Evaluation Criteria and Scale for "One in Four" Candidates

Evaluation Criteria	Evaluation Scale
Public Speaking:	1 = Stares at shoes, whispers, mumbles incoherently
• Eye contact	2 = Looks around the room, fidgets, restless
• Voice projection/clarity	3 = Tries for eye contact, projection/clarity lacking
• Mannerisms	4 = Good eye contact, clear, cogent, coherent
	5 = Polished, smooth, confident
	6 = Stellar, this guy could debate with Socrates
Candor:	1 = Profound lack of sincerity
• Openness	2 = Discussion of material is painful/overly difficult
• Sincerity	3 = Relatively at ease, maybe evasive, wishy washy
• Honesty	4 = More or less exudes openness and honesty
• Frankness	5 = Gives you a feeling of genuine sincerity
• Comfort	6 = Stellar—you feel like you've known this guy since birth
Appropriateness:	1 = Completely inappropriate
• Compassion	2 = Little sympathy, no concern of compassion
• Sympathy/Empathy	3 = Mildly indifferent, divided attention
• Sensitivity	4 = Warm, gentle, generally understanding
• Caring	5 = Truly empathetic, compassionate, entrusting
• Understanding	6 = Stellar—You would hope your sister would marry him

Passion Factor: 1 = Dead fish

- Commitment to the cause   2 = Would rather be doing something else

- Dedication to the group   3 = Under right circumstances would like to help

                                       4 = Excited, enthusiastic, ready to get started

                                       5 = He is deeply committed to the cause

                                       6 = Stellar—Five-alarm fire

Note: This page adapted from materials written by Andy Oldham.

Appendix E
The Men's Program
Training for University Judicial Boards*

We are members of the National Organization of Men's Outreach for Rape Education (NO MORE)—a group of educators working toward a day when there is no more rape and no more need for our organization.

Through conducting peer-education programs on college campuses for the past several years, our organization has developed a knowledge base valuable to campus judicial decision makers regarding sexual-assault cases. We want to share this knowledge with you as you prepare to adjudicate these types of cases.

Sexual assault of college students, particularly college women, is a major issue on college campuses today. A study of nearly 5,000 college students on 138 campuses around the country found that 20 percent of women and 4 percent of men reported that during their life they had been forced to have sexual intercourse against their will. Additional research has shown that one in four college women have experienced either rape or attempted rape since their fourteenth birthday.

Many survivors will seek campus disciplinary processes instead of, or in addition to, the criminal justice system. In fact, only about 5 percent of rape survivors say on surveys that they reported their rape to the police. So on college campuses, this leaves a lot of room for campus disciplinary processes to handle rape cases that don't go through the courts—and even to handle those that do. Sexual-assault cases will be among the most important and challenging cases you will hear as a hearing board member. Both because of the complexity of the cases and because the stakes are so high for the complainant and the accused. There are a number of reasons for this complexity including standards of evidence, privacy issues, and the resolution desired by both parties.

Overview

The objectives of this sexual-assault judicial training program are:

1. To help you understand how rape and sexual assault are defined in general, and specific to this campus.
2. To educate you about the prevalence of these types of incidents on college campuses.
3. To give you a clear idea what a rape experience might feel like.
4. To help you understand how a survivor is likely to react during and after a sexual assault.

---

*This chapter was coauthored with Andrea Perry, Director of Orientation and Judicial Affairs, Johns Hopkins University.

5. To educate you about some of the nature and prevalence of false reporting.

6. To teach you some common characteristics of perpetrators.

This knowledge base is intended to prepare you to make informed and sound decisions about the responsibility of the accused party or parties and, when necessary, to impose sanctions that appropriately address the needs of the accused, the complainant, and the university community.

Disclaimer

If you are a rape survivor, or are a friend or relative of a survivor, you may be particularly upset by our talk today, particularly by the videotape we will show you. If you'd like to talk more privately, we will be available at the end of the program. Also, just so you know, we have placed a pile of flyers by the door that give you an overview of resources available. Another option for you is to take advantage of support services available in the university counseling center.

Definitions

We'll begin by reviewing some basic definitions:

Criminal law and university conduct codes both address sexual assault, but may or may not use different terminology. In general, criminal statute separates rape from other types of sexual assault. In general these definitions apply.

The first definition we'd like to go over is for *sexual assault*. The definition we use for sexual assault is a broad one, and includes many different types of behavior. As you can see:

Sexual assault — sexual intercourse without consent, forcible sodomy, sexual penetration with an object, intentionally touching an unwilling person's intimate parts, or forcing an unwilling person to touch another's intimate parts. These acts occur by force, threat, surprise, intimidation, or by taking advantage of someone's helplessness or inability to consent.

So basically what this definition of sexual assault includes would be having sex with someone who doesn't agree to it or can't agree to it. It also includes oral sex, anal sex, penetrating someone with an object, touching someone's intimate parts or making them touch your intimate parts when they don't agree to do so and/or are forced to do so.

Rape is a more specific kind of sexual assault. According to the U.S. Department of Justice, the definition of rape is as follows:

Rape — sexual intercourse by force or against that persons will, or where the victim is incapable of giving consent given the person's age, or temporary or permanent mental or physical incapacity.

So you can see that rape would be having sex with someone when they don't agree to it or are forced into it, or are unable to agree to it. Cases of rape are also sexual assault, but not all sexual assault is rape.

Particularly in the case of rape, some people think that the most common type of rape happens when a rapist the woman doesn't know grabs her and rapes her somewhere. While rape by a stranger does occur sometimes, we want you to remember this:

Four out of five times when a woman is raped, it is by someone she knows. It could be an acquaintance. It could be a friend. It could be a date. But four out of five times, it is someone she knows. The average length of time she has known him is one year. Not just a few weeks, but on average, its been one year.

[Insert and review your university's sexual-assault definitions here.]

Your job is to enforce your university's code of conduct regarding sexual assault. As a hearing panel member, you need a thorough understanding of your university's policy regarding sexual assault. We'll give you some time now with your judicial officer to review that policy.

[Review the university sexual-assault policy here or in a separate session.]

After reviewing the law and the university's policy, you probably notice that your university's expectations for conduct may be different than that imposed by criminal law. Remember that it will be your task to determine whether the accused has behaved according to the university's expectations.

Empathy Exercise

Right now we're going to show you a 15-minute tape that describes a rape situation. This will help you understand what rape survivors go through. The tape itself is of a police trainer who is training new officers how to deal with rape situations. Again, we want to let you know that the video is graphic and disturbing. After the tape is over, we'll talk more about how it feels to be raped so you can better understand the perspective of a sexual-assault survivor.

[🎥 Show Tape Here]

We chose to use a videotape where a man rapes another man in order to demonstrate the dynamics of rape in a different way from what you might be used to hearing. We find that for those of us who have never experienced a sexual assault, particularly for men, this video helps us understand how powerless survivors tend to feel. Developing a capacity to empathize with a survivor's experience will help you make better judicial decisions.

A few things we need to point out. One is that the video is not intended to reinforce inaccurate stereotypes about male-on-male rape. In fact, what you heard here was a crime of violence, not a sexual act. As is the case with this video, research shows that many male-on-male rapes are committed by heterosexual aggressors. As we noted earlier, 20 percent of college women and four percent of college men report that in their lifetimes, they have been forced have sexual intercourse against their will. Both women and men on your campus have been victimized by sexual assault.

We will use this video to draw some parallels between the police officer's experience and common experiences women report having before, during, and after being sexually assaulted.

Police Officer's Experience

A Cop Moves a Trash Can

Think back to when the police officer decided to move the trash can. This was a normal part of his daily routine. There was no way to guess what was about to happen.

"Don't Make a Move"

In the next part of the video, the police officer is told not to make a move. His first reaction, as he is being threatened, is to remain still and figure out what is going on.

Get on Your Knees

Later, the police officer is told to get on his knees and it becomes more obvious what is about to happen. It's hard to tell what anyone would do in this situation, without living through it, but he decided the most important thing was to stay alive.

Experiences Common to Women

Everyday Situation Turns Bad

In the same way, many of the incidents in which women are raped arise out of normal everyday situations. A woman may go to the room of a trusted male friend or be with a guy she's met and would like to have some form of contact with, but then he takes control away from her. A nationwide research study found that 84 percent of rape survivors knew their attackers beforehand. Fifty-seven percent of rapes happen on dates. The point is that there are no big signals that a rape is about to occur, these are everyday situations that turn bad.

Overwhelming Fear

In a similar way, a rape victim's first instinct is to be scared and to freeze from the fear of what might happen. Usually, she's with someone that she trusts, and that trust is being violated. It is very common for her first reaction to be to remain absolutely still, and to freeze with an overwhelming sense of fear.

Desire to Avoid Violence

Men in general are much larger and stronger. Women can be intimidated and frightened by the sheer size of a man. Many women are socialized to avoid and to calm violent situations. They will often go along with what is happening to try to avoid violence to the extent possible. The average amount of force used is usually in the "moderate" range—usually twisting the victim's arm or holding her down. Only 9 percent are hit by their attackers, and only 5 percent are threatened with weapons. While many women (70 percent) do struggle physically, they end up being overpowered physically or psychologically.

Fear of STIs

In this situation, the police officer worried that given the high-risk contact that was involved, he had to worry about catching a whole variety of sexually-transmitted infections.

Fear of STIs and Pregnancy

Today, there are a lot of STIs to worry about. Today, being raped could mean catching a potentially fatal disease. According to the latest statistics one out of every 500 college student is infected with HIV. In addition, one out of five adults in the United States has genital herpes.

For women survivors, there is an added risk that men don't have. Women also face the possibility that the rape could have resulted in a pregnancy. They must then consider the ramifications of that pregnancy on their lives.

Humiliating Hospital Visit

Remember how he felt in the waiting room? He wasn't the first one in because he wasn't a gunshot victim, and he wasn't in immediate danger of dying. He was then put on a table and had a doctor probing around his body collecting evidence. Clearly, this was an uncomfortable, humiliating exam.

Another Painful Process

Many women describe the rape exam they go through in the hospital as painful. Once more, another person is probing her body, this time to take physical evidence and treat her injuries. Many women describe a normal gynecological exam as uncomfortable. A rape exam feels worse, and happens right after one of the worst experiences of her life.

Many women who are raped aren't comfortable even seeking medical attention. Only 5 percent go to the police, only 5 percent go to rape-crisis centers. Surveys show that 42 percent of women who are raped tell no one at all. Women fear loss of privacy, unwanted parental involvement, not being believed, retaliation, and other potentially negative outcomes of reporting.

In addition, a rape survivor has endured a significant physical and emotional trauma and often responds by doing nothing in an effort to pretend the assault did not occur.

Did You Fight?

Remember how the officers reacted to the raped officer. They couldn't believe he didn't fight back. They couldn't understand that he was just was trying to stay alive. They also suggested it might have happened before and maybe he really wanted it to happen.

Did You Resist?

Many people ask the woman if she resisted, if she fought back, where she was, whether she was drinking, what she wore at the time. The point is these things don't matter, she did not give consent, she was forced, and followed her instincts to avoid further harm. And no matter what, no one asks to be raped.

This rape experience we just described is similar to what many women experience in college. In fact, one out of every four college women have survived rape or attempted rape since they turned 14. One out of four college women have gone through an experience similar to the one we just talked about.

Rape-Trauma Syndrome

We've talked a lot about what the rape experience itself might be like. Now we want to talk about what the recovery period tends to be like. This recovery period tends to follow a pattern of what's known as "rape-trauma syndrome."

The impact of rape-trauma syndrome frequently deters a survivor from making a disciplinary complaint immediately after an incident. Rape-trauma syndrome also can create confusion for the complainant about what responsibility, if any, she had for the incident. Your job as a hearing panel member is to familiarize yourself with the ways in which rape-trauma syndrome can impact a survivor so that you can assess the credibility of her complaint in an accurate context.

We'd now like to give you a handout about rape-trauma syndrome. [Distribute Handout #10 from *The Men's Program* and give participants time to read over the handout.] The next thing we'd like to do is to lead you through an interactive exercise. We'll start by dividing you into four different groups [have people count off 1, 2, 3, 4; 1, 2, 3, 4, etc; have groups separate out into the four corners of your room]. For this exercise what we'd like you to do is for the 1's to take stage 1, the 2's to take stage 2, and so on. Each group should do two things. First, write a one- or two-paragraph narrative statement on what a rape survivor might say in that stage of rape-trauma syndrome. Second, write down some thoughts about how you think a woman in this stage of rape-trauma syndrome would respond to a police officer or university judiciary investigator who asked her questions about her rape experience.

[Give groups time to finish. Have each group report back to the larger group, process issues as necessary and as you have time to do so. As part of this processing, you may want to ask participants to compare and contrast what women might say at different stages of rape-trauma syndrome about their rape experience—when are more details likely to come out, when might she downplay the experience, when might she not want to go into it?]

False Accusations

We have to keep in mind that understanding rape-trauma syndrome does not equip you to know whether in any specific case a complainant is telling the truth about a sexual assault. False accusations do occur, although research indicates they represent a very small percentage of complaints to both the criminal justice system and to university judicial offices. Research by the FBI shows that 8 percent of rape cases reported to police are found to be not true. Thus, this indicates that 92 percent of the time, cases reported to the police are deemed credible, 8 percent of the time they are termed false reports.

Characteristics of Offenders

Research over the past 10 years has been able to provide us with a rough profile of college-age men who engage in forced sex. The handout we are passing out now enumerates several of those characteristics. Just because someone has many of these characteristics, does not make him guilty of any particular incident. However, these characteristics make it more likely for men to commit acts of sexual aggression and may also make men less likely to recognize their acts as sexually aggressive.

[Distribute Handout #17.]

A little more than halfway down the page, you'll see it says, "Are unable or unwilling to define their behavior as sexually coercive." This characteristic may mean that an accused student may truly believe he did not rape or otherwise sexually assault a woman when, according to policy or the law, he really did. Thus, a perpetrator may believe he was not coercive, and he may believe he is telling the truth in saying this, when in reality his behavior was coercive. It may explain why hearing panels are so often faced with a "he said, she said" scenario.

With all that you now know about sexual assault, rape-trauma syndrome, and about the characteristics of perpetrators, you still will need to evaluate each specific case in terms of the information presented to you in the hearing room.

To arrive at a determination of responsibility for a sexual assault, the hearing panel must determine:

1.   that a sexual encounter occurred between the complainant and the accused;

2.   that sufficient force was used by the accused; and

3.   that inadequate consent was given by the complainant.

Your conduct code may or may not establish specific definitions of force and consent. If these terms are defined, you should review these definitions with your judicial officer and understand them thoroughly. If your code does not define these terms, you should work with your judicial officer to understand your university's expectations, based on precedent, community, and conduct board values.

In establishing the facts of an alleged assault, the hearing must focus on issues of force and consent, assuming sexual contact happened. As the complainant and accused state their versions of what occurred, and as you question them and any witnesses, two of the most important things you must determine is that sexual contact occurred and that it occurred by either force and/or lack of consent.

As you know, most acquaintance-rape incidents occur when one or both of the people involved have been drinking or using other drugs. Research has shown that 75 percent of the men and 55 percent of the women were drinking or using drugs at the time a sexual assault occurred.

When questioning victims and perpetrators, you may want to consider asking some of the questions concerning the role of alcohol. Under criminal law, and under all student conduct codes which we have reviewed, if the aggressor is drunk or on drugs, he is still responsible for obtaining consent. He is also not excused from using force "just because he was drunk or high" and believed he could not control himself. In addition, we must keep in mind that if the alleged victim is intoxicated, she is incapable of giving proper consent. Thus, if the victim is drunk, an aggressor can be held responsible for sex without proper consent.

We'd like to leave you with one final statistic. In 2003, 179,000 women were victims of rape, attempted rape, or sexual assault. That's 20 women every hour. We've been here about an hour. If this was an average hour in this country, while we sat here, 20 women had an experience similar to the one you saw on the video.

Twenty-six women have been sexually assaulted. Twenty-six women have had an experience similar to the one we showed you on that video. Twenty-six best-friends, 20 sisters, 20 daughters. Twenty-six women have been sexually assaulted.

Thank you for your attention today. We wish you luck in your work as you thoughtfully separate truth from fiction, hold those responsible accountable for their actions, and as you work to make a difference on this important issue.

Appendix F
Condensed Training Program for Peer Educators

Recognizing that you may be unable to implement the full 45-hour training program to train your peer educators, this appendix offers some suggestions as to how you can train peer educators in 15 hours. Though this format is not ideal, it is enough to get the basic essentials covered to prepare peer educators to go out and present *The Men's Program*.

If you are on a traditional academic calendar and you plan to implement the 15-hour training program, it is suggested that you recruit peer educators in September, select them in October, and begin training on a Saturday in November. You will give your peer educators homework to do over the holiday break (as described below). Training will then conclude on a Saturday and Sunday in January. Your peer educators can then be ready to present in February. It is suggested that you begin with one or two "debut performances" in February, where you invite key programmers on your campus (fraternity and sorority presidents, residence-life staff, athletic team captains, key administrators and faculty) to preview the program for their organizations. This is also a great time to give women the opportunity to see a performance that is usually done in an all-male environment. You may also want to issue a press release regarding these debut performances. In some cases, simple press releases about this kind of debut has led to groups being the top story on three local network television news shows.

A training agenda for a 15-hour (three-day) training program is outlined below, including a large homework assignment.

Training Day 1

🕐 1:00 Introductions

1.   Introduce yourself and talk about your background and interest in sexual-assault issues.

2.   Set a ground rule that what is said in the room stays in the room (particularly with regard to personal information people discuss or sensitive opinions they share).

3.   Have each group member introduce himself stating his name, major, year in school, and clubs and organizations of which he is a member.

🕐 1:30 Setting the tone

1.   Indicate that the purpose of the group will be to present *The Men's Program.*

2.   Let peer educators know who is sponsoring the group. Review with them the fact that they will learn to present *The Men's Program.*

3.   Talk about the nature and benefits of using this program.

4.   Let them know what a potential office structure might look like for the group and what your role will be as the advisor.

🕐 1:45 Team building

1.   Ask participants to share two things with the group: Why he is here, and the strengths he believes he brings to the group.

🕐 2:15 Seeing *The Men's Program*

1.   Show your peer educators a full-length presentation of *The Men's Program.* If possible get peer educators who have presented *The Men's Program* before to present to your trainees. If this option does not work, another option is to use the video described in Appendix B to show your peer educators the program. An additional option is for you to learn the program yourself and/or with a colleague and present it to the class.

🕐 3:15 Discussion of reactions to *The Men's Program*

1.   Process reactions to the program by using the questions listed in Session 3.

🕒 3:45 Why is *The Men's Program effective?*

Using Handouts #12, #21, and #25 teach your peer educators about the research and theories underlying *The Men's Program* and the outcomes assessment research demonstrating its effectiveness. Use this as a chance to let peer educators know that there is scientific proof that what they will be presenting is effective, and that to date it is the most effective program published in the research literature. Use this handout to show peer educators how effective *The Men's Program* is, particularly in relation to other programs.

🕐 4:15 Who Is to Blame for Rape?

1. Have two volunteers present the skit in Handout #7.

2. Process this scenario using Handout #8.

🕟 4:45 Consent and Force

1. Teach peer educators about consent and force using the curriculum for Session 7.

🕜 5:30 Review Packet of Materials to Learn over Holiday Break

1. Distribute "To-Do List to Finish Before the Spring Semester." Review each item and see if there are any questions.

2. Next, divide the group in half. Call one half of the group "Team 1" and the other half "Team 2." Let them know that each team should learn half of the script according to their assigned team. Instruct them over the holiday break to practice this extensively so that they know it well enough to present without referring to the script as much as possible. Be sure to make copies of the articles and order the books they have to read to distribute at this time.

🕕 6:00 End

To-Do List to Finish Before the Spring Semester

1. Read, practice, and memorize as fully as possible your role in *The Men's Program* as a member of Team 1 or Team 2. I can't emphasize strongly enough how much time this takes and how much practice is needed. This is hard. Give it serious thought and time over break. Practice regularly, frequently, and give it serious time.

2. Read and study *The Men's Program* book. The most critical parts are Chapter 1, Handout #10, and Handout #14. To the extent possible, memorize the facts on Handout #14. These facts will help you answer the difficult questions, and will make you much more knowledgeable.

3. Read these four articles – Foubert 2000 *(Journal of American College Health)*, Foubert 2000 *(NASPA Journal)*, Malamuth 1981, and Koss, Gidycz, and Wisniewski, 1987. Know them well enough to be able to answer questions like:

    ■   How do you know *The Men's Program* works? What effects does it have on men? How do these effects compare to other programs? (both Foubert articles)

    ■   What is "likelihood of raping," how is it measured, what kinds of men are likely to rape? (Malamuth 1981)

    ■   Where does the one in four statistic come from? How do you know it is true? (Koss, Gidycz, and Wisniewski 1987)

4. Read "I Never Called it Rape" by Robin Warshaw. It goes by quickly, yet is very meaningful.

5. Read and study these portions of *The Men's Program:*
    Chapters 5 and 6, Appendix A, Handouts #6, #15, #16, and #17.

6. Read everything else in your training packet as provided.

Training Day 2

🕐 10:00 Overview and Team Building

1. Provide peer educators with an overview of the next two days of training.

2. Read the four questions from Session 2. Ask each group member to respond to one of the four questions as a team builder.

🕐 10:30 Sexual Assault in Context: Gender and Sexism

1. Use the discussion questions from Sessions 5 and 10 to facilitate a group discussion on gender and socialization as a context for sexual assault. As an additional resource, use Handout #17.

🕐 12:00 Lunch Break

🕐 1:00 Training: How to Handle Difficult People and a Variety of Questions

1. Go over Handout #15 "The More Interesting Responses We Get From Male Audiences," Handout #23 "How to Handle Difficult People and Questions," Handout #24 "Suggested Answers for a Variety of Questions" and Handout #14 "What Every Sexual-Assault Peer Educator Should Know." Take the class members through each handout. Encourage questions throughout. Ask them for alternative ways of answering the questions and/or dealing with the challenges. Ask them for personal experiences of how they may have dealt with questions and/or presenting situations that are similar to this before.

🕐 2:00 Role Play: How to Handle Difficult People and Questions

1. Before this portion of training, recruit five volunteers who are not members of the class to act out parts, as described in Handout #11. Meet with them as a group a few days beforehand to go over their roles and make sure they know what to do.

2. To start off, teach class members how to set up a room for a presentation by arranging the seating facing the presenters, checking the TV/VCR for a picture, testing the sound from the back of the room, etc.

3. Let the scene in Handout #11 play out, assigning members of the class, one by one, to tackle the challenges presented to them by the role players.

🕞 **3:30 Practice Presenting**

1. Put peer educators in pairs with one member from "Team 1" and one member from "Team 2" in each pair.

2. Assign one of the four portions of the program to each pair (part A, B, C or D).

3. Let them know that they will present this portion of the program to the rest of their peer educators tomorrow. (They should have already practiced all four parts assigned to their team over the holiday break, so this shouldn't be that difficult.)

4. Put each pair in their own room and give them time to practice presenting the portion they will present to the group tomorrow. If they finish, suggest they practice the rest of the program as well.

5. Walk around to each location and give them pointers and feedback on their presentations.

🕓 **4:15 Rape Trauma Syndrome**

1. Use Handout #10 and the exercise described in Session 17 to facilitate a discussion of rape-trauma syndrome.

🕔 **5:00 Sexual Assault and Alcohol**

1. Use the training exercise in Session 12 to facilitate a discussion of sexual assault and alcohol.

🕕 **6:00 End of Day**

Training Day 3

🕐 12:30 Ice Breaker/Team Builder

- Ask each group member to share the one thing they hope they will do as a group together in the coming year (present to every fraternity on campus, present to a certain portion of men on campus, whatever).

🕐 1:00 Homophobia and Male-on-Male Rape

- Facilitate a values clarification exercise regarding issues of homophobia by using Handout #2.

- Next, use Handout #22 to guide a discussion on using a male-on-male rape scenario in rape-prevention programming.

- Finally, have them look over Appendix A, Study 3, and talk them through the rationale for the study and the results.

🕑 2:00 Sexual-Assault, Nurse-Examiner Programs and Date Rape Drugs

1. Invite a SANE nurse in to talk about how rape survivors are cared for in hospitals and what an evidence collection exam is like.

2. Have the nurse provide an overview of date-rape drugs.

🕒 3:00 Present "The Men's Program" and Receive Feedback

1. Have each pair of peer educators present their part (A, B, C, or D) of *The Men's Program* to the entire group with their partner from yesterday.

2. During this exercise, have each peer educator write down feedback for each of their peers on a 3 x 5 card or piece of paper. Once each pair finishes presenting, ask for verbal critiques of each peer from the rest of the group. Give peer educators a chance to give their written feedback to each of their peers at the end.

🕟 4:30 In Her Own Words: What It's Like to Be a Survivor

1. Invite a rape survivor to training to tell her story. Pay close attention to issues of confidentiality. Set the proper tone in the beginning of class. If the survivor feels comfortable taking questions, set the proper tone for this discussion—what is said in the room stays in the room, she can "pass" on any question, etc. Make sure that every person in the class has at least one question ready for the survivor, to avoid an awkward silence when she asks if there are any questions.

🕟 5:30 Closing exercise

1. Have a closing exercise that wraps up the training experience, empowers the group members to make a difference, and increases group cohesion and morale. Make certificates for each member signed by you and perhaps another notable figure on your campus or institution.

2. Set a regular meeting time for the group to get together on a weekly basis.

🕕 6:00 End

Appendix G
References

Berg, D. R. "The Use of Rape-Specific Empathy Induction in Rape Education for College Men: A Theoretical and Empirical Examination" (unpublished master's thesis). University of Illinois, Urbana-Champaign.

Berg, D. R., K. A. Lonsway, and L. F. Fitzgerald. "Rape-Prevention Education for Men: The Effectiveness of Empathy-Induction Techniques." *Journal of College Student Development* 40 (1999): 219–34.

Berkowitz, A. D. *Men and Rape: Theory, Research, and Prevention Programs in Higher Education.* San Francisco: Jossey Bass, 1994.

Brecklin, L. R., and D. R. Forde. "A Meta-analysis of Rape Education Programs." *Violence and Victims* 16 (2001): 303–321.

Breire, J., and N. M. Malamuth. "Self-Reported Likelihood of Sexually Aggressive Behavior: Attitudinal Versus Sexual Explanations." *Journal of Research in Personality* 17 (1983): 315–23.

Burt, M. R. "Cultural Myths and Supports for Rape." *Journal of Personality and Social Psychology* 33 (1980): 217–30.

"Date Rape" Drug—Rohypnol. The National Women's Health Information Center. The Office on Women's Health. U.S. Department of Health and Human Services.

Davis, T. C, G. Q. Peck, and J. M. Storment. "Acquaintance Rape and the High School Student." *Journal of Adolescent Health* 14 (1993): 220–24.

Douglas, K. A. et al. "Results From the 1995 National College Health Risk Behavior Survey." *Journal of American College Health* 46 (1997): 55–66.

Earle, J. P. "Acquaintance Rape Workshops: Their Effectiveness in Changing the Attitudes of First Year College Men." *NASPA Journal* 34 (1996): 2–18.

Eby, K. K., J. C. Campbell, C. M. Sullivan, and W. S. Davidson. "Health Effects of Experiences of Sexual Violence for Women with Abusive Partners." *Health Care for Women International* 16/6 (1995): 563–76.

Ellis, A. L., C. S. O'Sullivan, and B. A. Sowards. "The Impact of Contemplated Exposure to a Survivor of Rape on Attitudes Toward Rape." *Journal of Applied Social Psychology* 22 (1992): 889–95.

Federal Bureau of Investigation. *Uniform Crime Reports.* Washington, D.C.: United States Department of Justice, 1995.

Fitzgerald, N., R. Fitzgerald, and K. Jack. "Drug Facilitated Rape: Looking for the Missing Pieces." *National Institute of Justice Journal* (April 2000).

Fonow, M. M., L. Richardson, and V. A. Wemmerus. "Feminist Rape Education: Does It Work?" *Gender and Society* 6 (1992): 108–21.

Foubert, J. D. "The Longitudinal Effects of a Rape-prevention Program on Fraternity Men's Attitudes, Behavioral Intent, and Behavior." *The Journal of American College Health* 48 (2000): 158–63.

Foubert, J. D., and S. L. LaVoy. "A Qualitative Assessment of 'The Men's Program:' The Impact of a Rape-Prevention Program on Fraternity Men." *NASPA Journal* 38 (2000): 18–30.

Foubert, J. D., and K. A. Marriott. "Overcoming Men's Defensiveness Toward Sexual Assault Programs: Learning to Help Survivors." *Journal of College Student Development* 37 (1996) 470–72.

Foubert, J. D., and K. A. Marriott. "Effects of a Sexual Assault Prevention Program on Men's Belief in Rape Myths." *Sex Roles* 36 (1997): 257–66.

Foubert, J. D., and M. K. McEwen. "An All-Male, Rape-Prevention, Peer-Education Program: Decreasing Fraternity Men's Behavioral Intent to Rape." *Journal of College Student Development* 39 (1998): 548–56.

Gilbert, B. J., M. Heesacker, and L. J. Gannon. "Changing Men's Sexual Aggression-Supportive Attitudes: A Psychoeducational Intervention." *Journal of Counseling Psychology* 38 (1991): 197–203.

Gray, N. B., G. J. Palileo, and G. D. Johnson. "Explaining Rape Victim Blame: A Test of Attribution Theory." *Sociological Spectrum* 13 (1993): 377–92.

Greenfeld, L. A. *Sex Offenses and Offenders: An Analysis of Data on Rape and Sexual Assault*. Washington D.C.: U.S. Department of Justice, Bureau of Justice Statistics, 1997.

Groth, N. A., and A. W. Burgess. "Male Rape: Offenders and Victims." *American Journal of Psychiatry* (1980): 137.

Grube, J. W., D. M. Mayton, and S. J. Ball-Rokeach. "Inducing Change in Values, Attitudes, and Behaviors: Belief System Theory and the Method of Value Self-Confrontation." *Journal of Social Issues* 50 (1994): 153–73.

Hamilton, M., and J. Yee. "Rape Knowledge and Propensity to Rape." *Journal of Research in Personality* 24 (1990): 111–22.

Heppner, M. J. et al. "The Differential Effects of Rape Prevention Programming on Attitudes, Behavior, and Knowledge." *Journal of Counseling Psychology* 42 (1995): 508–18.

Homes, M. M., H. S. Resnick, D. G. Kilpatrick, and C. L. Best. Rape-Related Pregnancy: Estimates and Descriptive Characteristics From a National Sample of Women. *American Journal of Obstetrics and Gynecology* 175 (1996): 320–24.

Kilmartin, C. Personal communication, 2000.

Kilmartin, C. *Sexual Assault in Context*. Holmes Beach, Fla.: Learning Publications, Inc., 2001.

Kilpatrick, D. G., R. Aciern, H. S. Resnick, B. E. Saunders, and C. L. Best. "A Two-year Longitudinal Analysis of the Relationships Between Violent Assault and Substance Use in Women." *Journal of Consulting and Clinical Psychology* 65/5 (1997): 834–47.

Kilpatrick, D. G., C. N. Edmunds, and A. K. Seymour. *Rape in America: A Report to the Nation*. National Victim Center, (1992).

Kilpatrick, D. G., C. L. Best, L. J. Veronen, A. E. Amick, L. A. Villeponteaux, and G. A. Ruff. "Mental Health Correlates of Criminal Victimization: A Random Community Survey." *Journal of Consulting and Clinical Psychology* 53/6 (1985): 866–73.

Koss, M. "Rape on Campus: Facts and Measures." *Planning for Higher Education* 20 (1992): 21–28.

Koss, M. P. and Heslet, L. "Somatic Consequences of Violence Against Women." *Archives of Family Medicine* 1 (1992): 53–59.

Koss, M. P., C. A. Gidycz, and N. Wisniewski. "The Scope of Rape: Incidence and Prevalence of Sexual Aggression and Victimization in a National Sample of Higher Education Students." *Journal of Consulting and Clinical Psychology* 55 (1987): 162–70.

Koss, M. P., L. Hiese, and N. F. Russo. "The Global Health Burden of Rape." *Psychology of Women Quarterly* 18 (1994): 509–37.

Lee, L. "Rape Prevention: Experiential Training for Men." *Journal of Counseling and Development* 55 (1987): 100–01.

Little, Kristin. "Sexual Assault Nurse Examiner (SANE) Programs: Improving the Community Response to Sexual Assault Victims." *OVC Bulletin*. Office for Victims of Crime, Office of Justice Programs, U. S. Department of Justice, (April 2001).

Lisak, D., and P. M. Miller. "Repeat Rape and Multiple Offending Among Undetected Rapists." *Violence and Victims* (in press).

Lonsway, K. A. "Preventing Acquaintance Rape Through Education: What Do We Know?" *Psychology of Women Quarterly* 20 (1996): 229–65.

Malamuth, N. M. "Rape Proclivity Among Males." *Journal of Social Issues* 37 (1981): 138–57.

McIntosh, P. "White Privilege and Male Privilege: A Personal Account of Coming to See Correspondences Through Work in Women's Studies," Working Paper No. 189. Wellesley College. Center for Research on Women, 1988.

National Center for Injury Prevention and Control. *Rape Fact Sheet.* Atlanta: Centers for Disease Control and Prevention, U.S. Department of Health and Human Services.

National Victim Center and Crime Victims Research and Treatment Center. *Rape in America: A Report to the Nation* 1992.

O'Sullivan, C. "Acquaintance Gang Rape on Campus." In A. Parrot and L. Bechhofer (eds.) *Acquaintance Rape: The Hidden Crime.* New York: John Wiley and Sons. (1991): 140–56.

Peterson, S. A., and B. Franzes. "Correlates of College Men's Sexual Abuse of Women." *Journal of College Student Personnel* 28 (1987) 223–28.

Petty, R. E., and J. T. Cacioppo. *Communication and Persuasion: Central and Peripheral Routes to Attitude Change.* New York: Springer-Verlag, 1986.

Rennison, C. M. "National Crime Victimization Survey, Criminal Victimization 2000: Changes 1999–2000 with Trends 1993–2000." Washington, D.C.: U.S. Department of Justice, Bureau of Justice Statistics, NCJ 187007, 2001.

Resnick, H.S., Acierno, R., and D. G. Kilpatrick. "Health Impact of Interpersonal Violence 2: Medical and Mental Health Outcomes." *Behavioral Medicine* 23 (1997): 65–78.

Sanday, P. R. *A Woman Scorned: Acquaintance Rape on Trial.* University of California Press: Berkeley: 1996.

Sanday, P. R. "Rape-Prone Versus Rape-Free Campus Cultures." *Violence Against Women* 2 (1996): 191–08.

Scarce, M. "Same-sex Rape of Male College Students." *Journal of American College Health* 45 (1997): 171–73.

Scarce, M. *Male-on-Male Rape: The Hidden Toll of Stigma and Shame.* New York: Insight, 1997.

Schewe, P. A., and W. O'Donohue. "Sexual Abuse Prevention with High-Risk Males: The Roles of Victim Empathy and Rape Myths." *Violence and Victims* 8 (1993): 339–51.

Schewe, P. A. *Guidelines for Developing Rape-Prevention and Risk-Reduction Interventions: Lessons from Evaluation Research.* Paper presented to the Illinois Coalition Against Sexual Assault, June 1999.

"Sexual Abuse of Boys." *Journal of the American Medical Association.* December 2, 1998.

Simon, T. B., and C. A. *Harris. Sex Without Consent: Peer Education Training for Colleges and Universities*, Vol. 2. Holmes Beach, Fla.: Learning Publications Inc., 1993.

Thompson, S. "Behavioral Profile of Acquaintance Rapists." Paper presented at the Tenth International Conference on Sexual Assault and Harassment on Campus. Orlando, Fla., (October 2000).

Tjaden, P., and N. Thoennes. "Prevalence, Incidence, and Consequences of Violence Against Women: Findings From the National Violence Against Women Survey," 2–5, Research in Brief, Washington, D.C.: National Institute of Justice, U.S. Department of Justice, 1998.

U.S. Department of Justice. *Victim Costs and Consequences: A New Look*, 1996.

U.S. Department of Justice. "Bureau of Justice Statistics Report on Crime Victimization in 1998."

Virginians Aligned Against Sexual Assault. *Rape Trauma Syndrome*. Paper presented at the Meeting of Virginians Aligned Against Sexual Assault. Richmond, Va.: November 1992.

Warshaw, R. *I Never Called It Rape*. New York: Harper Collins, 1994.